INTO THE FIRE

STORIES OF HEROISM FROM OCTOBER 7

For sales inquiries, contact: store@israel365.com

Into the Fire: Stories of Heroism from October 7 was produced by Israel365.

Cover Design by Sara Lamm and Yehudit Weingarten
Typeset by the Virtual Paintbrush

ISBN: 978-1-957109-61-9, softcover
ISBN: 978-1-957109-62-6, hardcover

First Edition 2024

www.Israel365.com

ISRA£L365

INTO THE FIRE

STORIES OF HEROISM FROM OCTOBER 7

SARA LAMM

TABLE OF CONTENTS

GRAPPLING WITH LOSS: LOOKING TOWARDS THE FUTURE

RABBI TULY WEISZ, FOUNDER OF ISRAEL365

As the first anniversary of October 7 approaches, it is hard to grapple with the reality that a year has passed since the great tragedy. On the one hand, October 7 feels like it happened yesterday, yet at the same time, it seems like a nightmare out of the darkest periods of ancient Jewish history. After a horrific year of grief, terror, violence and hatred directed towards our people, how are we supposed to remain upbeat and positive about the future? The answer lies in the pages of this book.

Alongside the suffering Israelis have endured this year, we have witnessed awe-inspiring stories of self-sacrifice, courage and resilience. Instead of running away in fear, hundreds of thousands of brave IDF soldiers ran into the fire. Rather than hunkering down to protect their own families, Israeli citizens dropped everything to serve as reservists, medics and volunteers.

In this spirit we offer *Into the Fire: Stories of Heroism from October 7* as a unique opportunity for reflection and inspiration. Our enemies are filled with hate, but our nation is full of love. They destroy, but we build. The wicked terrorists of Hamas, Hezbollah and Iran glorify death and hide behind their women and children, while our brave nation fights a righteous and moral war for the entire world to see.

The defence of our people extends beyond the courageous IDF soldiers. These stories showcase a wide range of heroism: from the all-women's Tank Unit that fought tirelessly for over 17 hours on October 7, to non-Jewish supporters who advocate for and defend Israel, to the parents of fallen soldiers who, despite their loss, continue to provide strength to their families and the nation of Israel with remarkable dignity.

This book would not have been possible without the devotion of Sara Lamm, Rabbi Elie Mischel, Shira Shechter and Rabbi Rami Goldberg. Since October 7, the entire dedicated staff of Israel365 has worked overtime to defend Israel by being a force for truth and light in this dark world.

The heroic acts described in *Into the Fire: Stories of Heroism from October 7* are a testament to the enduring spirit of the Jewish people. While we may not yet understand the full scope of God's plan for Israel, these stories of bravery and sacrifice offer a powerful glimpse into the resilience and greatness that lies within. It is our fervent hope that this strength will soon radiate from Israel, inspiring and enlightening the entire world.

ACKNOWLEDGEMENTS

This book, *Into the Fire*, owes its existence to the invaluable contributions of many. I wish to express my deepest *Ha-Karat HaTov* (gratitude) to Shira Schechter, Rabbi Elie Mischel, Rabbi Tuly Weisz, and Rabbi Rami Goldberg for their talents and dedication in bringing this project to fruition. Special thanks to Yehudit Weingarten for her exceptional work on the book design.

I am profoundly grateful to the passionate team at Israel365 for their unwavering support throughout this endeavor. Their commitment has been instrumental in making this book a reality.

To all who shared their stories and to those who helped in any way, your contributions are deeply appreciated. This book stands as a testament to your collective efforts and the spirit of collaboration that made it possible.

This book brings together the stories of the heroes of October 7, whose extraordinary acts of courage, bravery, and dignity emerged in the face of overwhelming hatred. The horrors of that day were unimaginable, yet these individuals rose above the darkness. To the heroes featured in these pages: You shouldn't need a book written about you; you should be living your daily lives, free from the terror that thrust you into the spotlight. This book is dedicated not only to you but also to the hundreds of thousands of heroes—in Israel and around the world—who risk their lives every day in support of the Jewish people, the Hebrew Bible, and the State of Israel.

Thank you, God, for bringing these stories to light, allowing us to learn from them, and for always watching over and protecting Israel.

May we all find the hero within.

IN DEDICATION

The horrific plight of the hostages and the tragic loss of so many loved ones serving in the IDF has cast a heavy shadow over Israel. Yet, even in this darkness, there is a glimmer of hope. We are united by our shared heritage and faith in the Bible, which guarantees a positive outcome for Israel while warning of consequences for those who stand against her and God's chosen people.

While many books are written to inspire, entertain, inform, or motivate, *Into the Fire: Stories of Heroism from October 7* stands in a category of its own. It tells the stories of heroes and heroines who selflessly defended Israel during one of the darkest periods in its history since the Holocaust. It illuminates darkness with light and kindles hope, and Tikvah, for the future of Israel and the Jewish people worldwide.

I pray that the narratives within these pages will inspire others to heed the "calling of the land" under God's Covenant promise and consider making Aliyah to stand united with their brothers and sisters in One Jewish State. Am Yisrael Chai!

A heartfelt thank you to Sara for using her God-given talents and dedication to share the stories of those who bravely went *Into the Fire*!

DEBBIE AND THOMAS COPE

Elie Wiesel once spoke about the importance of speaking to Holocaust survivors, saying "To listen to a witness is to become a witness."

Out of the horrors of October 7, a light shone in the darkness—the light of ordinary people doing the extraordinary. Laying down their own lives to save others is the greatest triumph one can accomplish in this life.

The rescuers and the rescued bear witness to the events of October 7, and it is imperative that their stories are heard and passed down from generation to generation. History is a powerful teacher.

My late mother and father bore witness to the atrocities of World War II, and throughout our lives, they carefully shared some of their experiences, which profoundly shaped us. My mother and I visited Yad Vashem in Israel, but as we stood at the entrance, my dear mother was so overwhelmed with emotion that she chose not to go inside. Her tears told me all I needed to know; though years had passed, the pain and memory of that period were as real as ever.

I stand witness today, and it is to my parents, Dorthy and Malcom, that I dedicate this testament and give thanks.

GABRIELLA SOMERVILLE

We are honored to dedicate this book to our three boys, Caden, Cole and Connor. May they grow into mighty men of God and positively impact the lives of others. May the gifts that God has given them grow and flourish as they age, may they forge fiercely forward in faith despite their challenges and may they overcome and prove that our God has the final say.

JASON AND MONIQUE LANG

"But the people devoted to their God will stand firm" (Daniel 11:32) Dedicated in in memory of Matilda Asa, Lavena Hawley, and Levana Konforty.

DAWN KONFORTY

May Hashem bless and watch over all our Heroes of October 7 ,and may He comfort the families and loved ones of those who have fallen.

With much love and prayers,

RICK AND PATRIZIA NEEL

Hashem & Am Yisrael Chai!

DONNA JOLLAY & JERUSALEM TOURS

HEROES OF THE ISRAEL365 COMMUNITY

PLATINUM

- Awelani Malange
- Debbie Cope
- Donna Jollay
- Dawn Konforty
- Gabriella Somerville
- Monique & Jason Lang
- Monique Leendertz

GOLD

- Angela Sokol
- Christine Zelm
- Denise Wood
- Donna Lauria
- Esther Brumit
- Gail Carlson
- Gordon Shaw
- Hal Bryan
- Jan Moorman
- Jayant Thorat
- Judy Rogers-Lavigne
- Kelly Kohen
- Lesley Silberstein
- Lisa Zaloudek
- Linda Given
- Margareta Lazin
- Matt Matthews
- Richard Flournoy
- Roberta Plaat
- Sarah MacGill
- Simon Ealson
- Steven Geurtsen
- Tracy Flaherty
- Yuhsiu Chung

HEROES OF THE ISRAEL365 COMMUNITY

INTRODUCTION

BIBLICAL HEROISM AND WHAT BEING A HERO MEANS TODAY

INTO THE FIRE: OCTOBER 7, 2023

On the morning of October 7, 2023, Israel awoke to a day that will forever scar its national psyche. What began as a peaceful Shabbat and the joyous holiday of Simchat Torah, the final day of the Feast of Tabernacles quickly descended into unimaginable terror and tragedy.

In the early hours of the morning, Hamas terrorists launched a multi-pronged attack on southern Israel. The scale and brutality of the assault were unprecedented. Thousands of rockets rained down on Israeli towns and cities while armed terrorists breached the Gaza border fence, infiltrating nearby communities, military bases, and even a music festival.

The terrorists targeted civilians indiscriminately, tearing families apart as they murdered and took hostages. The Nova music festival, a celebration of peace and unity, became a scene of horror as heartless Hamas terrorists gunned down and abducted young people in the prime of their lives. Kibbutzim and small towns, long symbols of Israel's pioneering spirit, became battlegrounds.

The toll was devastating. Over 1,100 Israelis were murdered, making it the deadliest day in Israel since the country's founding as well as the deadliest mass killing of Jews since the Holocaust. Thousands more were injured, and about 240 people were taken hostage to Gaza. Since October 7, Israel's death toll has continued to rise, with hundreds of soldiers and civilians killed due to fighting in Gaza and from ongoing Palestinian terrorism in northern Israel and Judea and Samaria., The physical destruction has been extensive, with homes, schools, and entire communities left in ruins.

The psychological impact was equally profound. The October 7, attack shattered the sense of security that many Israelis had come to take for granted. The brutality of the assaults, which included horrific acts of torture, sexual violence, and the slaughter of children and babies, left deep emotional scars on survivors and the nation as a whole.

The events of October 7, and its aftermath reshaped the geopolitical landscape of the Middle East. They also sparked a global conversation about antisemitism, as hundreds of thousands of rioters across the world called for the destruction of Israel and the murder of Jews.

Yet, amidst this horrible darkness, sparks of light continue to illuminate. Stories of incredible bravery, selflessness, and resilience began to surface. Ordinary people performed extraordinary acts of heroism, risking their lives to save others. Communities came together, transcending religious and ethnic divides to support one another.

It is against this backdrop of tragedy and courage that the stories in this book unfold. Each account of heroism is set against the stark reality of that terrible day and its aftermath. These are not just tales of individual bravery, but testimonies to the human spirit's capacity to rise from the ashes of unthinkable horror.

By reading and sharing these stories, we honor the memory of those lost, stand in solidarity with those who suffered, and celebrate those who, in humanity's darkest hour, chose to be a light.

Heroism is as old as humanity itself. We find countless examples of individuals who stood tall in the face of overwhelming odds, whose actions shaped the course of history and inspired generations to come. These biblical heroes, much like their modern counterparts, were not always born into greatness. They were ordinary people who, faced with extraordinary circumstances, chose to act with unwavering conviction and selflessness.

When we study the lives of these biblical heroes, we learn that the essence of heroism transcends time. The same qualities that defined the heroes of old – courage, sacrifice, quick thinking, and moral fortitude – are mirrored in the actions of those who rose to the occasion during and after October 7. From paramedics to soldiers, from survivors to those who made the ultimate sacrifice, each story in this book is a testament to the enduring nature of human bravery.

Let us begin our journey by examining four exemplary figures from the Hebrew Bible: Esther, Jonathan, Jael, and Phinehas. Though separated by centuries, their narratives intertwine, teaching us what it means to be a true hero.

ESTHER: THE QUEEN WHO RISKED EVERYTHING

In the Book of Esther, we encounter a young Jewish woman who finds herself in a position of great influence as the queen of Persia. When Haman, the king's advisor, plotted to annihilate the Jewish people, Esther was faced with a monumental choice. She could remain silent, protecting her own life but abandoning her people, or she could risk everything by approaching the king uninvited – an act punishable by death – to plead for her people's lives.

Mordecai's message to his niece Esther captures the essence of her heroism:

"For if you remain silent at this time, relief and deliverance will arise for the Jews from another place, and you and your father's house will perish. And who knows whether you have not attained royalty for such a time as this?" (Esther 4:14).

At this pivotal moment, Esther chose to act. Her famous response, "If I perish, I perish" (Esther 4:16), reflects a willingness to sacrifice herself for the greater good. Esther's heroism lies not in physical strength or battlefield prowess but in her moral courage and strategic thinking. She used her position, intelligence, and faith to save her people from genocide.

Esther's story is one of calculated risk, unwavering faith, and the courage to speak truth to power when the stakes could not have been higher. It resonates with modern heroes who find themselves in positions where they must choose between personal safety and the greater good. Like the diplomats who spoke out against injustice or the journalists who risked their lives to report the truth in the aftermath of October 7, Esther's legacy lives on in those who use their voice and influence to protect the vulnerable.

JONATHAN: THE HERO OF FRIENDSHIP AND LOYALTY

The story of Jonathan, son of King Saul, presents us with a different kind of heroism – one rooted in friendship, loyalty, and the courage to do what is right, even when it conflicts with personal interests or familial expectations.

Jonathan's heroism is most evident in his relationship with David, the man chosen by God to succeed Saul as king. Despite being the heir apparent to the throne, Jonathan recognized David's divine appointment and chose friendship and righteousness over power and position.

The depth of Jonathan's loyalty is beautifully captured in this passage:

"Then Jonathan made a covenant with David because he loved him as himself. Jonathan stripped himself of the robe that was on him and gave it to David, with his armor, including his sword and his bow and his belt"(I Samuel 18:3-4).

This act of giving David his princely robe and weapons was more than a gesture of friendship; it was a symbolic abdication of his claim to the throne. Jonathan's heroism lies in his ability to see beyond his own interests, to support a friend, even when it means giving up his own ambitions.

Moreover, Jonathan repeatedly risked his life to protect David from Saul's murderous intentions. He stood up to his father, the king, advocating for David's life and innocence:

> *"Let not the king sin against his servant David, since he has not sinned against you, and since his deeds have been very beneficial to you"* (I Samuel 19:4).

Jonathan's courage in confronting injustice, even when it came from his father, exemplifies a heroism that is as relevant today as it was thousands of years ago. His story reminds us of the heroes who, in the wake of October 7, set aside personal gain or safety to help others – the neighbors who sheltered strangers, the friends who risked their lives to save companions, and those who spoke out against hatred and violence, even when facing backlash from their own communities.

JAEL: THE UNEXPECTED HEROINE

The story of Jael, found in the Book of Judges, presents us with an unexpected hero – a woman who, through quick thinking and decisive action, changed the course of Israel's history. Jael's heroism came at a crucial moment during a war between the Israelites and the Canaanites.

Sisera, the commander of the Canaanite army, fled from battle and sought refuge in Jael's tent. Despite the alliance between her husband's family and Sisera's, Jael recognized the opportunity to aid the Israelites and end the oppression her people had suffered.

The Bible describes her actions with stark simplicity:

> "But Jael, Heber's wife, took a tent peg and seized a hammer in her hand, and went secretly to him and drove the peg into his temple, and it went through into the ground, for he was sound asleep and exhausted. So he died" (Judges 4:21).

Jael's heroism lies in her bravery, quick thinking, and decisive action. She saw an opportunity and seized it, despite the personal risk and the unconventional nature of her actions.

The prophetess Deborah later praised Jael in song:

> "Most blessed of women is Jael, the wife of Heber the Kenite. Most blessed is she of women in the tent" (Judges 5:24).

Jael's story resonates with modern heroes who find themselves in unexpected situations requiring immediate action. She reminds us of the civilians who, on October 7, and in its aftermath, acted swiftly and decisively to save lives. These ordinary people became extraordinary through their quick thinking and courage.

Jael's heroism also challenges our preconceptions about what a hero looks like. She was not a warrior, a leader, or someone in a position of power. She was an ordinary woman who, when faced with an extraordinary situation, chose to act heroically. This echoes the stories of many modern heroes – the paramedics, the volunteers, the passersby who, in moments of crisis, step up and make a difference.

PHINEHAS: THE ZEALOT FOR RIGHTEOUSNESS

Phinehas, the grandson of Aaron the High Priest, presents us with a more controversial form of heroism – one driven by a zealous commitment to moral and religious principles. His story, found in the Book of Numbers, showcases a moment of firm resolve in the face of moral decay.

When the Israelites began to engage in immoral behavior with the Moabites, incurring God's wrath and a deadly plague, Phinehas took dramatic action:

> *"When Phinehas the son of Eleazar, the son of Aaron the priest, saw it, he arose from the midst of the congregation and took a spear in his hand, and he went after the man of Israel into the tent and pierced both of them through, the man of Israel and the woman, through the body. So the plague on the sons of Israel was checked"* (Numbers 25:7-8).

While Phinehas' actions may seem extreme by modern standards, the ultimate Judge conferred His blessing upon him. The Bible records God's approval:

> *"Phinehas, the son of Eleazar, the son of Aaron, the priest, has turned away My wrath from the sons of Israel in that he was jealous with My jealousy among them so that I did not destroy the sons of Israel in My jealousy"* (Numbers 25:11).

Phinehas's heroism lies in his unwavering commitment to his principles and his willingness to act to defend them in a moment of crisis. His zeal for righteousness and quick response to threats against his people's moral and physical well-being earned him a "covenant of peace" and a lasting priesthood.

In the context of modern heroism, Phinehas's story reminds us of those who stand firmly for their principles, even in the face of danger or social pressure. During moments of crisis like the attack of October 7, we desperately need the brave men and women who stand up against injustice, hate, and moral corruption – often at significant personal risk.

THE COMMON THREAD: FROM BIBLICAL HEROES TO MODERN VALOR

As we reflect on these four biblical figures – Esther, Jonathan, Jael, and Phinehas – we begin to see the common threads that connect their ancient heroism to the modern heroes we encounter in the pages that follow.

1. **Courage:** Each of these biblical heroes demonstrated remarkable courage. Esther risked her life by approaching the king uninvited. Jonathan stood up to his father, the king, to protect his friend. Jael took on a powerful military commander. Phinehas acted boldly in the face of moral decay, risking a punishment of death if his actions were, in fact, misguided. This same courage is evident in the stories of those who, on October 7, and in its aftermath, ran towards danger to save others,

stood up against hatred, or persevered through unimaginable loss.

2. **Quick Thinking and Decisive Action:** Our biblical heroes acted quickly and decisively. This mirrors the actions of modern heroes – the first responders who made split-second decisions to save lives and the civilians who improvised solutions in crisis situations.

3. **Moral Conviction:** Each of these ancient heroes was driven by a strong sense of what was right. Esther's commitment to her people, Jonathan's loyalty to his friend, Jael's determination to aid the Israelites, and Phinehas's zeal for righteousness all reflect a deep-seated moral conviction. Today's heroes often display this same unwavering commitment to their values, standing up for what they believe is right even in the face of danger or social pressure.

4. **Sacrifice:** The willingness to sacrifice for a greater cause is a hallmark of heroism. Esther risked her life, Jonathan gave up his claim to the throne, Jael risked retribution, and Phinehas put himself in harm's way. This spirit of sacrifice is mirrored in the actions of those who, in the wake of October 7, put the needs of others before their own safety or comfort.

5. **Unexpected Heroes:** None of these biblical figures were born knowing they would become heroes. They were ordinary people who, faced with extraordinary circumstances, chose to act heroically. This is perhaps the most powerful connection to modern heroism – the recognition that heroes often emerge from the most unexpected places.

DEFINING THE MODERN HERO

In bridging the gap between these ancient tales and the contemporary stories that fill the pages of this book, we realize that the essence of heroism remains constant across the ages. Like the heroes of the Bible, modern heroes are not born knowing they are going to have a heroic mission. Rather, heroes are people who, presented with moments of challenge and opportunity, stick to their convictions and act with courage, compassion, and selflessness.

The heroes of October 7, and its aftermath embody these qualities. They are the paramedics who rushed into danger to save lives, echoing Jael's quick thinking and bravery. They are the ZAKA volunteers who, with dignity and respect, tended to the deceased, reflecting the moral conviction of Phinehas. They are the lone soldiers who left the comfort of their homes to defend the land they love, mirroring Jonathan's loyalty and sacrifice.

We see modern Esthers in the diplomats and public figures who used their positions to advocate for justice and peace, risking their reputations and sometimes their safety to speak truth to power. We find echoes of Jonathan's friendship in the stories of those who sheltered their neighbors, regardless of background or belief, during times of danger.

The heroes in this book include those who survived harrowing injuries on October 7, demonstrating a resilience that would make the biblical heroes proud. We honor those who made the ultimate sacrifice, protecting others with their final acts of bravery. We celebrate the non-Jews who stood up for Israel, showing a moral courage that transcends national and religious boundaries.

These modern heroes remind us that heroism is not about perfection or invincibility. It's about ordinary people making extraordinary choices in moments of crisis or need. The biblical heroes were not superhuman; they were flawed, complex individuals who chose to act with courage and conviction when it mattered most. In the same way, the heroes of October 7, and its aftermath are not mythical figures but our neighbors, friends, and fellow citizens who, in the crucible of crisis, revealed the best of humanity.

This book is more than a collection of heroic tales. It is a testament to the enduring human spirit, a reminder that in our darkest hours, the light of courage, compassion, and hope shines brightest. As we read these stories, we are challenged to ask ourselves: What would we do in similar circumstances? How can we cultivate the qualities of heroism in our daily lives?

In truth, heroism is not just about grand gestures or moments of high drama. It's also about the small acts of kindness, the daily choices to stand up for what's right, and the ongoing commitment to build a better world. As we turn the page to explore these remarkable stories, let us remember that heroes are not born, but made– by circumstance and by their own will. And let us be inspired to nurture the seeds of heroism within ourselves, ready to answer the call when our moment comes.

In the end, the greatest tribute we can pay to the

heroes of October 7, and its aftermath, and to all the heroes who have come before, is to let their courage inspire our own.

CHAPTER ONE

HEROIC LEGACY: ELCHANAN KALMANSON

"Then I heard the voice of the Lord saying, 'Whom shall I send? And who will go for us?' And I said, 'Here am I. Send me!'"
(Isaiah 6)

"It doesn't look good," he told his parents and wife, "and I need to go and help." His brother Menachem and nephew Itiel joined him. They jumped in their car and drove towards the Gaza border to the unknown.

Capt. (res.) Elchanan Kalmanson wasn't supposed to be at Kibbutz Be'eri on the morning of October 7, 2023. He was supposed to be 49 miles away, together with his family in the town of Otniel. But when the unthinkable happened, when Hamas terrorists breached the border and began their brutal massacre of innocent civilians, Elchanan made a choice that would alter the course of many lives - and ultimately cost him his own. With his brother Menachem and nephew Itiel by his side, Elchanan embarked on a rescue mission that would push the boundaries of human bravery and self-sacrifice. His story would come to symbolize the indomitable spirit of a nation under siege and remind us of the extraordinary courage of "ordinary" people faced with unimaginable horror.

Elchanan Meir Kalmanson was born in the community of Otniel in southern Judea, not far from the holy city of Hebron. From an early age, he exhibited qualities of leadership, bravery, and an unwavering commitment to his community and country. His parents, Benny and Yochi, played a significant role in shaping his character. They were pillars of the community, actively involved in various social and religious activities. Benny, a respected rabbi, often shared stories of the great heroes of Jewish history with his children, instilling in them a powerful sense of duty and pride.

Elchanan's childhood was filled with moments that, in retrospect, hinted at his future heroism. He was an avid reader, often engrossed in books about historical battles and figures who had shaped the course of Jewish and Israeli history. His siblings recall a young Elchanan organizing mock rescue missions in their backyard, rallying his friends and siblings to "save" imaginary captives. These childhood games were more than just play; they were the early signs of his strategic thinking and his deep-seated desire to protect and to serve - even if he didn't know it yet.

His education was both traditional and progressive. Elchanan attended the local yeshiva (religious Jewish school), where he excelled in his studies, particularly in subjects related to Jewish law and history. His teachers remember him as a diligent student, always eager to learn and quick to help his classmates. Outside of school, he was involved in various community service projects, often leading efforts to clean up local parks or organize charity drives.

As Elchanan grew older, his commitment to service became more pronounced. After completing his mandatory military service, he voluntarily continued serving in the Israeli security services. His exact roles and missions remain classified to this day, but it is known that he was involved in numerous high-stakes operations that required not only physical courage but also keen intelligence and strategic acumen.

One of his notable contributions was his work in developing combat training guides for local security teams. These guides were instrumental in training thousands of security personnel nationwide, equipping them with the skills and knowledge needed to protect their communities effectively. Elchanan's dedication to this work was evident in the meticulous detail and practical advice contained in these guides.

Beyond his professional duties, Elchanan was a leader in his community. As the head of security for Otniel, he was responsible for the safety of his fellow residents, a role he took very seriously. He organized regular training sessions, ensuring everyone knew what to do in an emergency. His proactive approach to security earned him the respect and admiration of his neighbors.

His father, Benny, often spoke about Elchanan's

willingness to step up wherever help was needed. "Anyone who knew Elchanan even a little knew that this was the most natural thing in the world, that wherever help was needed, wherever leadership, devotion, thoughtfulness, and bravery were called for, wherever there weren't enough people — Elchanan was there." This sentiment was echoed by many in the community, who saw in Elchanan a leader who led by example.

On October 7, news of the Hamas invasion spread rapidly, reaching Elchanan early in the morning. Given his role as head of security and his extensive experience, he quickly grasped the severity of the situation. He told his parents and wife, "It doesn't look good, and I need to go and help."

Elchanan's brother, Menachem, and his nephew, Itiel, shared his sense of urgency. They, too, felt a deep need to act. Though none of them had been officially called up for reserve duty, the three men decided to head to the front lines.

Their destination, Kibbutz Be'eri, was the largest kibbutz in the Gaza envelope. Home to around 1,100 residents, it was under severe attack by Hamas terrorists. The usually peaceful community had been transformed into a battlefield, with smoke rising from burning homes and the air filled with the sounds of gunfire and explosions.

The journey to Kibbutz Be'eri was fraught with danger. As Elchanan, Menachem, and Itiel drove toward the Gaza border, they encountered scenes of chaos and destruction. All around them, thousands of rockets were being fired into Israel, and the roads were filled with people fleeing the violence. Despite the danger, they drove on, driven by the urgency to help those in dire need.

Upon arriving at Be'eri, Elchanan's extensive training in anti-terror security operations became crucial. He quickly assessed the situation and devised a plan to evacuate the residents. The army had special forces on the ground, working to secure the perimeter, but the terrorists had already taken control of many homes. The only way to save people was to go from house to house, a perilous task that required immense bravery and quick thinking.

Elchanan, Menachem, and Itiel took an armored truck and began their mission. They encountered numerous challenges, including resistance from terrified residents who feared that opening their doors would expose them to terrorists posing as IDF soldiers to trick them into leaving their safe rooms. To reassure them, Elchanan would recite the Shema Yisrael prayer, a powerful testament to their shared faith and identity.

"Listen, Israel! Hashem is our God, Hashem is One."
(Deuteronomy 6:4)

This act of faith convinced the residents that they were indeed being rescued by fellow Jews, allowing Elchanan and his team to evacuate them to safety.

For 14 grueling hours, Elchanan and his team went from door to door, rescuing over 100 people. They faced numerous dangers, including direct confrontations with terrorists. In many instances, they had to kill terrorists before they could rescue the residents. Despite the risks, they continued their mission with unwavering determination, driven by the knowledge that many lives depended on their actions.

In one particularly harrowing instance, they arrived at a house engulfed in flames. Inside, they found a family trapped in a safe room. Despite the intense heat and smoke, Elchanan and his team managed to break through the door and evacuate the family. The parents and their three children were saved.

On October 8th, as Elchanan and his team continued their mission to clear Be'eri of remaining terrorists, they entered one final home. Inside, they were ambushed by a terrorist hiding in a corner of the house. Elchanan shouted 'I've been hit' and fell near the entrance of the house, where he lost consciousness. Soon afterward, the IDF arrived and provided cover, allowing Elchanan to be evacuated to a field hospital. Tragically, he died before he could be evacuated by helicopter.

Elchanan was buried on October 12th in Otniel. Thousands came to pay their respects and honor his memory at his funeral. His father spoke at the funeral, highlighting Elchanan's unwavering dedication and bravery. "In our family," Benny said, "we laugh about everything—this is well known. I apologize—but after seeing the dedication of all those who organized the funeral, I have to say that Elchanan would have done it much better."

His wife, Shlomit, recounted their 20 years together,

filled with shared joy, challenges, and dreams for the future. The loss was deeply felt by all who knew him, but his legacy of courage and selflessness left an indelible mark on their hearts. "I wanted forever with you," she said at his funeral. "We dreamed of how we would grow old together and what we would do over the years. We had so many plans for our long lives... You were my rock. You always knew immediately, what I needed in any situation. You loved the children so much and you were so proud of them... For you, family was the highest value."

Elchanan's heroism received due recognition. The group he led that fateful day, dubbed "Elchanan's team," was awarded the Israel Prize for civilian heroism. This prestigious honor, announced by Education Minister Yoav Kisch, acknowledged the extraordinary bravery and sacrifice demonstrated by Elchanan, Menachem, and Itiel. The decision to dedicate that year's prize exclusively to civic heroism and societal responsibility in light of the war against Hamas, underscored the exceptional nature and profound impact of their actions.

The award ceremony evoked mixed emotions for Elchanan's family. His wife Shlomit expressed both pride and profound grief, reflecting on Elchanan's deep love for his country and how deserving he was of this recognition. "I received the news with mixed emotions - excitement, longing, and pride. There is a tremendous sense of excitement here. Elchanan loved the country so much, and he truly deserves to receive this prize. This is his place in the chain of generations of the people of Israel. On a personal level, he is sorely missed."

His cousin, Orit Marek, praised his heroism and lamented that he could not be there to receive the award himself. "It's emotionally overwhelming and so sad that Elchanan is not here. The number of people who are alive today is incomprehensible - thanks to him and because of them. I am proud of them for their noble act on that cursed Saturday. With extraordinary courage, they saved entire families. I wish Elchanan were here to receive the prize too. I am proud of Shlomit, his wife, and the children, who also deserve this prize."

Education Minister Yoav Kisch highlighted the broader significance of Elchanan's actions and the award. "We are a nation of heroes. Let us not forget that," Kisch said. "It was an honor for me to speak this morning with the families of Menachem Kalmanson and Itiel Zohar and inform them about the prize being awarded. I thanked them for their wonderful family and the incredible heroes who emerged from their midst, serving as a beacon of bravery for all of us and a source of unity and national pride."

Elchanan's heroism was not an isolated event within his family. His cousin, Lt. Pedayah Mark, fell in battle in the Gaza Strip shortly after Elchanan's death. Pedayah's father, Elchanan's uncle, was murdered in an Arab terror attack in 2016. This pattern of bravery and sacrifice highlights the family's deep commitment to the safety and security of Israel. The Kalmanson family's legacy of service and sacrifice is a testament to their unwavering dedication to their country.

Elchanan's actions on October 7, and 8 resonated

deeply within Israeli society. His story quickly symbolized unity and courage, transcending the political and social divides that often fragment the nation. The residents of Be'eri, a secular kibbutz, expressed their eternal gratitude to the Kalmanson family, recognizing the sacrifice Elchanan, a religious Jew, made to save their lives. His act of heroism bridged the gap between different segments of Israeli society, highlighting the shared values and common humanity that bind them together.

During the seven-day mourning period, members of Kibbutz Be'eri visited the Kalmanson family to express their gratitude and share stories of how Elchanan had saved their lives. These visits were emotionally charged, with many residents breaking down in tears as they recounted the moments Elchanan rescued them from certain death.

Elchanan's story also resonated with the broader Israeli public. His actions were widely covered in the media, and his heroism became a rallying point for a nation grappling with the trauma of the Hamas invasion. Public figures and community leaders cited Elchanan's bravery as an example of the selflessness and unity that define the Israeli spirit. His story was used to foster a sense of national pride and resilience, reminding Israelis of their shared values and the importance of standing together in the face of adversity, even though the country had been deeply divided in the months leading up to the Hamas attack.

In the aftermath of Elchanan's death, his wife, Shlomit, continued his legacy by advocating for a strong and uncompromising stance against Hamas. Speaking before the Knesset House Committee, she emphasized the need for a firm and unyielding approach to ensure the safety and security of Israel. She also highlighted the importance of not repeating past mistakes, such as the lopsided prisoner exchange deals that led to the release of terrorists like Yahya Sinwar, who later became the mastermind behind the October 7, massacre.

Shlomit's voice in the Heroism Forum, an apolitical group of bereaved families, unifies the collective call for continued vigilance and strength. In her speeches, Shlomit often draws upon her personal experiences and the values that Elchanan embodied. She speaks about the importance of national unity and the need for all Israelis to come together in defense of their country. Her words resonate with many, as she has articulated a vision of strength and resilience rooted in the shared values of courage, dedication, and love for one's country.

Elchanan Kalmanson's life was a testament to courage, dedication, and selflessness. His actions during the Hamas invasion of southern Israel not only saved lives but also inspired a nation. His legacy lives on through his family and the countless people he touched through his heroism. Elchanan's story serves as a powerful reminder of the impact one individual can have and the enduring spirit of unity that binds the people of Israel.

CHAPTER TWO

HEROIC WOMAN OF VALOR: HADAS LOWENSTERN

What a rare find is a capable wife!
Her worth is far beyond that of rubies.
Proverbs 31:10

"Talking about his death is secondary. He only died once. He lived every day. He literally grabbed every second. And I am alive and my six kids are alive and this is our plan: We plan on living a wonderful life. We'll live. We'll live in *Eretz Yisrael* (land of Israel) and be a happy Jewish family. And this is the true victory."

On December 13, 2023, the seventh day of the Jewish festival of Hanukkah, Hadas Lowenstern's life changed forever. Her beloved husband, Elisha Lowenstern, was killed in Gaza while serving as a reservist in the Israel Defense Forces (IDF). Elisha, a 38-year-old American-Israeli, was part of a tank crew sent to rescue wounded soldiers in southern Gaza. Tragically, the tank was hit by an anti-tank-guided missile fired by Hamas, claiming

Elisha's life and leaving Hadas a widow with six young children.

The night Hadas found out about Elisha started like any other. The warm glow of the Hanukkah candles flickered across the festive table, casting dancing shadows on the faces of the gathered family. Laughter filled the air, mingling with the aroma of latkes and the sweet scent of sufganiyot. Hadas, her eyes twinkling with joy, watched as children took in the beautiful Hanukkah lights.

Then came the knock at the door.

Three sharp raps, cut through the merriment like a knife. Instinctively, anyone who has a spouse, brother, son, daughter, or loved one fighting in the Israeli army, knows what those knocks mean. As she opened the door, the sight of three solemn IDF officers standing on her threshold made her heart plummet. Their presence, a harbinger of devastating news, was all it took for her world to begin crumbling.

Time seemed to slow as they delivered the words that would forever divide her life into "before" and "after." Elisha, her beloved, her partner, her children's father - gone. The officers' voices faded into a muffled drone as the reality of their message crashed over her like a tidal wave.

In that instant, Hadas felt as if she were standing on the edge of an abyss, teetering between the warmth of the life she knew and the cold, dark unknown that now stretched before her. Yet, even as she felt herself being torn apart by shock and grief, steadfast part of her refused to be swept away. It was as if a switch had been flipped, activating a reserve of strength she didn't know she possessed. The sounds of her children's laughter, now painfully bittersweet, pierced through her shock, anchoring her to the present.

To understand Hadas Lowenstern's extraordinary response to tragedy, one must first understand her journey and the values that have shaped her life. Born and raised in Netanya, Israel, Hadas grew up in a warm, non-religious family. She is the ninth generation of her family to live in Israel, a fact that has deeply influenced her connection to the land and its people.

As a young adult, Hadas served in the IDF, where she had her first encounter with a religious Jew. This experience sparked a journey of self-discovery and exploration of her Jewish heritage. Intrigued by the profound wisdom she discovered in Judaism and the Bible, Hadas spent three years studying Torah in a post-high school institution for women. It was during this time that she decided not just to study the Bible, but to live it.

This spiritual journey led Hadas to meet Elisha Lowenstern, an American-Israeli who had made Aliyah (immigration to Israel) with his family at the age of 8. Despite their cultural differences, Hadas was immediately struck by Elisha's interpersonal qualities, particularly his ability to listen and truly care about others. Their shared values and commitment to their faith formed the foundation of their 13-year marriage and the family they built together.

Elisha and Hadas Lowenstern's home was filled with

love, faith, and purpose. They raised their six children with a deep appreciation for their Jewish heritage and a strong connection to the land of Israel. Elisha, described by Hadas as "such a good man," was known for his kindness, attentiveness, and dedication to personal growth. In their home, every milestone was celebrated, every achievement acknowledged. Elisha would create special certificates for his children when they completed their study of a tractate of Talmud, fostering a love for learning and a sense of accomplishment. This positive atmosphere and emphasis on personal development were hallmarks of the Lowenstern household.

When war broke out on October 7, 2023, Elisha Lowenstern, though exempt from combat duty due to having six children, chose to volunteer. For Elisha and Hadas, this was not a decision to be debated but a clear call of duty—a privilege and the highest honor to defend their country. Elisha served in Gaza for ten weeks before his tank was hit by an anti-tank missile. His death was a devastating blow not only to his family but to his entire community. Yet, in the face of this immense loss, Hadas Lowenstern emerged as a source of strength and inspiration.

Within hours of receiving the news of her husband's death, Hadas decided to speak to the press. In the days and weeks following Elisha's death, she began sharing her thoughts and feelings through short videos and interviews. She had a message to share—one of strength, unity, meaning, and faith. This decision to turn her tragedy into a source of inspiration for others is one of the most remarkable aspects of Hadas' story. Her words, infused with a deep faith and an unwavering commitment to life, quickly resonated with people worldwide.

What makes Hadas's response to tragedy truly heroic is her ability to transcend her pain and grief to become a source of strength and inspiration for others. In the face of a loss that could have left her bitter and withdrawn, Hadas chose to reach out, to share her story, and to offer hope to those who might be struggling with their own challenges. This act of turning personal suffering into a force for good requires immense courage, selflessness, and a profound sense of purpose. Hadas's heroism lies not in denying her pain, but in choosing to channel it into a message that uplifts and strengthens others.

One of Hadas' most powerful messages is her perspective on life and death. She says, "Talking about Elisha's death is secondary. He only died once. He lived every day. He literally grabbed every second. And I am alive and my six kids are alive and this is our plan: We plan on living a wonderful life. We'll live. We'll live in Eretz Yisrael (the land of Israel) and be a happy Jewish family. And this is the true victory." Rather than being consumed by grief, Hadas chooses to focus on life, on the legacy her husband left behind, and on the future she is determined to build for her children. This choice to embrace life in the face of devastating loss is not just inspiring—it's heroic.

Central to Hadas's resilience is her deep faith. While she was not born into a religious family, her journey to Orthodox Judaism has provided her with a framework for understanding and coping with the challenges life has presented. Hadas often speaks about the concept of *emunah* (faith) and *bitachon* (trust in God). She emphasizes that these are not passive beliefs but rather active choices that require constant work and reinforcement. She compares developing faith to training for sports, saying that just as one needs to practice and work out to improve in athletics, one must put in time and effort to develop a deeper connection with God.

This faith allows Hadas to see beyond her immediate grief and to find purpose in her loss. She believes that everything happens for a reason, even if that reason is not immediately apparent. This perspective helps her to focus on what she can do in the present moment rather than being paralyzed by sorrow or anger. It's this ability to find meaning and purpose in the heart of her personal tragedy is what sets Hadas apart and makes her response so powerful and inspiring to others.

One of the most striking aspects of Hadas' response to her loss is her emphasis on gratitude. Even in her grief, she consciously chooses to focus on what she is thankful for rather than what she has lost. She often speaks about the privilege of having been married to Elisha for 13 years, of having six beautiful children, and of living in the land of Israel. She finds reasons to be grateful, comparing her situation to those who have lost young, unmarried children or who have no children at all, humbly recognizing that their loss may be even greater than her own.

This attitude of gratitude is not a denial of her pain

or loss but rather a conscious choice to find balance in her life and to acknowledge both the sorrow and the joy. As she puts it, "Every time I want to break down and feel bitter, I say to myself, 'Listen, you have six kids – say thank you!'" The beauty in this is that her children have internalized this attitude as well. In their own ways of memorializing their late father from showing kindness to others, and requesting communal prayer in his memory. This perspective is closely tied to her message about the importance of living life to the fullest. She often speaks about how Elisha made the most of every moment of his life, always striving to be a better person, a better neighbor and a better Jew. This commitment to personal growth and making a positive impact on the world is something Hadas continues to emphasize in her own life and in her message to others.

Another important aspect of Hadas' message is the significance of community and mutual support. She speaks openly about the help she receives from family, friends, and community members, emphasizing the importance of both giving and receiving kindness. This message of interdependence and community support is particularly poignant in a world of "bowling alone," when so many people lack the community support that our grandparents took for granted.

In addition to these personal reflections, Hadas also uses her platform to speak about the reality of life in Israel and the complexities of the ongoing conflict. She urges people to look beyond headlines and statistics to see the real human lives affected by the war.

While Hadas's strength and resilience are remarkable, she is always quick to acknowledge the challenges she and her children face. Each of her six children, ranging from a baby of 10 months to a thirteen year old boy is grappling with the loss of their father in their own way. Hadas approaches her children's grief with the same mix of faith, pragmatism, and compassion that characterizes her own response to loss. She allows each child to express their emotions in their own way, providing support and understanding as needed. She speaks of crying with her children, of hugging teddy bears named after their father, and of having one-on-one "dates" to give each child individual attention and space to share their feelings.

At the same time, Hadas strives to instill in her children the same sense of purpose and meaning that has helped her cope with their loss. She emphasizes the importance of their Jewish heritage, their connection to the land of Israel, and the values their father lived by. In this way, she ensures that Elisha's memory and legacy continue to shape and guide their family.

In the wake of her loss, Hadas Lowenstern has worked hard to share her husband's legacy with the world. She sees this as a divine mission, a way to keep Elisha's memory alive and to spread the values he lived by. Hadas speaks frequently about Elisha's commitment to personal growth, his kindness, and his dedication to his faith and his country. She shares anecdotes about his daily habits of self-reflection and improvement, his attention to detail in his relationships with others, and his unwavering commitment to his principles.

One story in particular captures their profoundly deep and spiritual relationship: something they lay the foundation for even at the beginning of their marriage.

In the midst of their wedding preparations, Hadas and Elisha found themselves at a tasting session with their caterer. The event was more a formality than a necessity for the young couple, whose minds were focused on their impending union rather than the menu details. As Hadas recounted later, with a bittersweet smile:

"We just wanted to get married, they could have served pizza for all we cared."

Yet it was during this seemingly mundane outing that Elisha chose to make a profound gesture. Taking a moment away from the chatter about appetizers and main courses, he penned a heartfelt note to his bride-to-be. Hadas's voice softened as she recalled the words:

"I, Elisha Halevi ben HaRav Tzvi Meir promise to love you always, in This World and the Next World."

She paused, her eyes misting over with the memory. "He signed his name at the bottom," she added.

Hadas then shared her initial reaction to this sweeping declaration:

"I said to him: 'How do you know? Things might change. Maybe you'll find out that I'm not such a great wife. How can you promise?'"

Her practical nature had momentarily overshadowed the romance of the gesture. But Elisha's response was unwavering:

"He said, 'I promise.'"

Hadas's voice filled with a mixture of pride and sorrow as she concluded:

"And he stood by his word."

Through her public speaking and media appearances, Hadas has become a voice not just for her own family, but for all those affected by the ongoing conflict. She puts a human face on the statistics of war, reminding the world of the real lives impacted by each loss. In doing so, she embodies a key element of her story: the focus on the power of choice. Despite the overwhelming tragedy she has faced, Hadas underscores that we are not powerless; we can choose how we respond to the situations life presents us.

Hadas chooses to find meaning in her loss rather than being consumed by grief. She chooses to continue living and building a future for her children rather than being paralyzed by the past. Hadas is open about her struggles, her moments of weakness, and the challenges she faces. But she consistently emphasizes that, although we cannot control what happens to us, we can control how we respond.

Hadas' story is not just one of personal tragedy and triumph. It reflects the broader Israeli experience of a people who have faced numerous challenges throughout history but continue to persevere, build, and hope for a better future. Nevertheless, the lessons she shares have universal relevance. Her focus on gratitude, resilience, community support, and finding meaning in difficult circumstances resonates with people of all backgrounds. And ultimately, her story challenges us to consider our own choices in how we respond to hardship and loss.

CHAPTER THREE

HEROICALLY ALONE: THE COURAGEOUS STORIES OF ISRAEL'S LONE SOLDIERS

"Two are better off than one, for they have greater benefit from their earnings. For should they fall, one can raise the other, but woe betide him who is alone and falls with no companion to raise him!"
Ecclesiastes 4: 9-10

"I am not going to wait for the world to do something great for me, I am going to do something great for the world" –Rose Lubin

Most 18 and 19-year-olds in Western countries spend the summer before college shopping at Target, decorating their dorm rooms, or taking road trips with friends to celebrate their newfound freedom. Having just graduated high school, the world is their oyster. But a select group of young adults uses that time to prepare for a very different type of adventure.

Instead of cozy dorms, they will sleep in sparse bunk rooms. Instead of carefree road trips, they carry heavy gear on grueling hikes, training for their service in the Israel Defense Forces (IDF). These young men and women from America, Canada, France, England, and beyond, voluntarily leave the comforts and safety of their homes to enlist in the IDF. Many of them come to Israel without their family in physical proximity. Many of them come to Israel, knowing very well the risk that they are taking in joining the IDF.

Their official title is "Lone Soldiers," but they are far from alone. They stand together, embodying a profound patriotism and unwavering belief that Israel should never fight alone.

ROSE ELISHEVA LUBIN: A ROSE PICKED FOR THE JOB

Rose Lubin's journey began in the vibrant Jewish community of Atlanta, where she grew up in a loving and supportive family. From a young age, Rose displayed a zest for life and a wide array of talents. She attended public school, actively participated in her local Jewish Student Union, and enjoyed her summers at Camp Nageela, a Jewish summer camp in New England. Rose was a true polymath: she excelled as a poet, playwright, illustrator, musician, singer, actress, and dancer. She was also a dedicated volunteer. Her high school years were marked by exceptional achievements, and her athletic prowess was equally impressive. She was a champion wrestler, varsity cheerleader, and an avid horse lover. Graduating from Dunwoody High School in 2021, she was academically brilliant and deeply committed to her Jewish faith and the State of Israel.

Rose's connection to Israel was evident from a young age. A trip to Israel with her grandfather at age four ignited a lifelong passion for the land and its people. By age eight, she was already talking about moving to Israel. This dream culminated in her making Aliyah immediately after high school, driven by a sense of duty and a desire to contribute to the Jewish state. Rose's parents, David and Robin, supported her decision wholeheartedly, understanding the deep conviction behind her choice. "You could die. You could give your life," Robin told Rose, recognizing the gravity of her daughter's commitment. But Rose, who dreamed of getting married and having seven children, responded with unwavering resolve, "Mom, if not me, it will be someone else."

Upon her arrival in Israel, Rose enlisted in the Israel Defense Forces (IDF), where she excelled in her training, graduating at the top of her class. She became a certified fitness instructor, helping other soldiers meet rigorous physical standards. Rose's commitment extended beyond basic training as she specialized in combat, focusing on anti-terrorism tactics. She was deployed as a border policewoman and trained to become an IDF commander. Rose could have chosen to be stationed anywhere in Israel, but she selected a particularly challenging assignment: guarding the Old City of Jerusalem. This historic and volatile area requires the utmost vigilance and bravery, as it is a frequent flashpoint for conflicts.

Rose's service was marked by her profound sense

of purpose. In a speech at the 2023 Friends of the IDF Dinner in Atlanta, she eloquently expressed her dedication: "There are generations of my family who could have been here today if there was an Israel during the Holocaust. I feel an obligation to them to fulfill the opportunities they didn't have. It's our duty to watch over the Jews who are living the dream of walking to the Kotel (Western Wall) on Shabbat (the Sabbath)."

The morning of October 7, 2023, began one of the darkest chapters in Israel's history. In the early hours of that painful day, Rose was off-duty, celebrating Simchat Torah with Idan and Tamar James, her host family at Kibbutz Sa'ad near the Gaza border. Many lone soldiers like Rose are paired with a family who takes them in, provides home-cooked meals when the soldiers are off duty, and generally becomes their adoptive family: a home away from home.

When the attacks began, Rose did not hesitate for a second. She immediately donned her uniform, grabbed her weapon, and joined the kibbutz's Rapid Response Team. For 14 hours, Rose stood at the kibbutz gate, a critical position that she defended with unwavering resolve. Her actions were instrumental in preventing Hamas terrorists from infiltrating Kibbutz Sa'ad, saving countless lives. The kibbutz was spared and her bravery and quick thinking allowed it to serve as a safe haven and a strategic point for IDF reinforcements.

Throughout the attack, Rose displayed remarkable courage and resilience. She assisted in rescuing injured civilians and evacuating them to safety while under fire.

Her quick thinking and decisive actions were crucial in mitigating the damage inflicted by the terrorists.

Despite the traumatic events of October 7, Rose's commitment did not waver. She returned to her duties with the Border Police in Jerusalem, insisting on resuming her post. Tragically, on November 6, 2023, Rose's life was cut short. A 16-year-old Palestinian Arab from the East Jerusalem neighborhood of Issawiya approached the border police officers stationed near Herod's Gate, brandishing a knife. He stabbed Rose multiple times and also injured another officer before being shot and killed by Rose's fellow officers. Both Rose and the other injured officer were taken to Hadassah Hospital, where Rose was pronounced dead several hours later.

The news of Rose's death sent shockwaves through her family, friends, and the wider community. Her funeral at Mount Herzl Cemetery in Jerusalem was a testament to the impact she had on those around her. Attended by thousands, including high-ranking military officials and fellow soldiers, the ceremony was filled with heartfelt tributes.

Her brother, Alec, eulogized her, recalling her strength and unwavering spirit. "Rose taught me to hold my head high, walk with a purpose, and to love those close to me with all my heart, always offer a hand and never to judge unfairly," he said. Her mother, Robin, read from Rose's Bat Mitzvah speech, which poignantly encapsulated her life's mission: "I am not going to wait for the world to do something great for me; I am going to do something great for the world."

Rose's life was a blend of seemingly contradictory qualities. She was both fierce and gentle, a warrior and an artist. Her rabbi from Atlanta, Rabbi Binyomin Friedman, described her as "color, music, skipping, laughing, painting, and writing. She was light itself."

Despite her small stature, Rose was a formidable presence. Her high school wrestling career, during which she reached the state finals as the only female on the team, showcased her determination and resilience. She carried this same tenacity to her military service, where she confronted challenges with unwavering resolve.

Rose's creativity and artistic talents were another integral part of her identity. She wrote award-winning compositions, created impressive works of art, and excelled in singing, acting, and dancing. Her father, David, highlighted this blend of qualities: "Rose was creative and passionate." At high school graduation, she was at the top of her class academically and the only graduate to letter in both wrestling and cheerleading.

From a young age, Rose stood up against injustice and bullying. Her father recounted how bullies in the area soon learned, to their regret, that a five-foot-tall girl was the toughest kid in the neighborhood. This courage extended to her military service, where she became known for her bravery in confronting potential threats in Jerusalem's Old City.

Rose's decision to join the IDF and serve in one of Israel's most challenging areas was driven by a profound sense of duty and a desire to make a difference. She saw herself as a protector of the Jewish people and the land of Israel. Her colleagues in the IDF and Border Police speak of her as someone who never backed down from a challenge, always smiling even in the most difficult circumstances.

Rose's legacy extends beyond her immediate circle. The Georgia General Assembly posthumously honored her with State Senate Resolution #11EX, and the United States Senate Judiciary Committee introduced Resolution 536 to honor her bravery and memory. The Steinhardt Foundation for Jewish Life established the Rose Lubin Jewish Pride Award, ensuring that her spirit of courage and dedication continues to inspire future generations.

Rose's life was a testament to the power of purpose and sacrifice. She lived with a clear sense of mission, dedicating herself to the protection of Israel and its people. Her story serves as a powerful reminder of the profound impact one person can have on the world and the sacrifices made by lone soldiers who leave their homes and families to serve Israel.

The lover of Judaism, the artist, the wrestler, the girl in funny clothes, the friend and confidante were all facets of a remarkable woman who walked with God while marching to the beat of her own drum. Rose saw the world as a place "with no boundaries, only endless opportunity." Her life, though tragically cut short, continues to inspire those who knew her and those who learn about her remarkable journey.

ILAN COHEN: A LONE SOLDIER'S JOURNEY OF HEROISM

Born and raised in Buenos Aires, Argentina, Ilan

Cohen was a young man with a profound sense of purpose and a deep-rooted Zionism that guided his decisions. After graduating from high school, Cohen made the life-changing choice to immigrate to Israel, a country he felt a strong connection to despite never having lived there. His journey began at the Karmiel absorption center in Israel, where new immigrants are welcomed and assisted in adjusting to their new home.

Cohen's commitment to integrating into Israeli society was evident in his educational pursuits. He attended Yeshivat Har Bracha, a hesder yeshiva (religious Jewish school) that combines traditional Talmudic studies with military service. This institution, located in the heart of Samaria, became a pivotal part of Cohen's life, where he immersed himself in religious studies and prepared for his future role in the IDF.

Rabbi Barel Shevach, one of Cohen's instructors at the yeshiva, spoke highly of his dedication and ability to integrate both socially and academically. Despite initial challenges with the Hebrew language, Cohen's perseverance and determination shone through. He was described as "fearless" and "Zionistic in every fiber of his being," qualities that would define his military career.

Cohen enlisted in the IDF's 202nd Battalion of the Paratroopers Brigade, specifically joining the Hetz Company. This unit, established in 2016, was designed to integrate Haredi and other strictly observant recruits into the elite special forces brigade. As a lone soldier, Cohen did not have a family in Israel to return to during furloughs, making his integration into the military community even more significant. By all accounts, Cohen was successful. His comrades and instructors noted his pleasant demeanor and his rapid adaptation to the demands of military life. In a tragic incident involving friendly fire, Sergeant Ilan Cohen was killed in action on May 15, 2024 in the northern Gaza Strip.

Yossi Dagan, the head of the Samaria Council, described Cohen as a hero both in life and death. He praised Cohen's bravery in leaving his homeland and family in Argentina to come to Israel, where he not only studied Bible but also dedicated himself to the security and protection of his adopted country. Cohen's commitment to his faith, his new homeland, and his fellow soldiers was a testament to his character and values.

Cohen's friends and fellow students at the yeshiva (religious Jewish school) remembered him as a sweet, gentle, and kind-hearted individual who was full of love and deeply Zionistic. Eitan Goldschmidt, a close friend, eulogized Cohen, highlighting his incredible efforts to immigrate to Israel, improve his Hebrew, and serve in the IDF. Goldschmidt's words captured Cohen's dedication and expressed the profound loss felt by those who knew him.

Yehuda Fisher, another friend from the yeshiva, reflected on Cohen's ultimate sacrifice for the sanctification of God and the protection of Israel. He described Cohen as a "supreme saint" to whom they owed everything. The sentiments shared by Cohen's friends and community painted a picture of a young man who was admired and respected for his unwavering commitment to his beliefs and his new homeland.

Ilan Cohen's story is one of courage, dedication, and sacrifice. As a lone soldier, his journey from Buenos Aires to Israel epitomizes the spirit of those who choose to defend a land they hold dear, despite the immense personal sacrifices involved. His legacy lives on in the hearts of those who knew him and in the collective memory of a nation that honors its heroes. The diversity of the communities that Cohen touched serves as a reminder of the unity and shared destiny that bind the people of Israel together.

Cohen's life and service stand as a powerful testament to the ideals of Zionism and the profound impact one individual can have on the world. His story will continue to inspire future generations of Israelis and Jews around the world, highlighting the enduring values of bravery, faith, and love for the land of Israel. May his memory be a blessing.

NATHANIEL YOUNG: A SACRIFICE FOR THE LAND HE LOVED

At the age of 20, Nathaniel Young made the ultimate sacrifice defending the country he had chosen to call home. His story is not just one of tragedy but of passion, dedication, and the pursuit of a deeply held dream.

Born and raised in London, Nathaniel was described by those who knew him as someone with an infectious zest for life. His sister, Gaby Shalev, spoke of his "selfless kindness" as a rare and precious quality. Coupled with a profound love for Israel, these qualities would shape the course of his life.

From a young age, Nathaniel felt a deep connection to Israel. This wasn't merely a passing interest but a calling that resonated within his soul. As he grew older, this connection only strengthened, ultimately leading him to make a decision that would change his life forever: to leave the comfort of his home in London and make Aliyah to Israel.

For many people, moving to a new country would be daunting enough. But Nathaniel's commitment went further. He chose to enlist in the IDF, joining the prestigious Golani Brigade as a lone soldier.

The life of a lone soldier is not easy. It requires tremendous courage, adaptability, and resilience. Yet, by all accounts, Nathaniel thrived in his new role. His brother Eliot recalled how Nathaniel had "found true happiness in Israel," a joy that was "infectious" to those around him.

Despite the demands of military service, Nathaniel remained deeply connected to his family. His siblings spoke of his generosity with his time, showering affection on his nephews and nieces during his periods away from duty.

The last time Eliot saw his brother was during the Jewish festival of Sukkot, just a week before the tragic events of October 7. They spent time together in Jerusalem's vibrant Machane Yehuda Market, engaging in deep discussions about faith. It was a moment of connection between brothers, punctuated by what Eliot called their "traditional big goodbye hug" as Nathaniel boarded the last bus home. Little did they know it would be their final embrace.

On October 7, 2023, Nathaniel was serving with his unit near the Gaza border and was among those who responded to the Hamas attack. In the chaos and violence of that day, Nathaniel made the ultimate sacrifice, giving his life in defense of the country he had come to love so deeply.

On a hillside in Jerusalem's Mount Herzl, Israel's national cemetery, thousands gathered to pay their final respects to Nathaniel. The funeral was a poignant reflection of the impact this young man had made in his short life. People from across Israeli society - religious and secular, military and civilian - came together to honor his memory.

Nathaniel's parents, having flown in from London, joined his four siblings, three of whom live in Israel. In the midst of their profound grief, they spoke of their immense pride in their son. Shontel and Nicky Young later shared, "His deep love for the country and unwavering commitment to its defense instill in us a sense of immense pride amid our profound sorrow."

The outpouring of support from the thousands who attended the funeral and paid respects during the shiva led his parents to decide to honor their son's memory in the most profound way possible: they chose to make Aliyah themselves, relocating to Netanya, Israel.

In explaining their decision, Shontel and Nicky said, "Nathaniel bravely and determinedly fulfilled his dream of defending the State of Israel. From the warmth and support we felt from thousands at the funeral and during the seven-day mourning period we realize that Israel is our new home."

This decision to follow in their son's footsteps and embrace the country he loved so dearly is perhaps the most powerful tribute to Nathaniel's legacy. It speaks to the depth of his commitment and the strength of the connection he felt to Israel—a connection so powerful that it has now drawn his family to make the same journey he did.

The Lone Soldier Center in Memory of Michael Levin, an organization that supports IDF soldiers serving without family in Israel, paid tribute to Nathaniel, saying, "His dedication, courage, and sacrifice will forever be etched in our hearts. May his memory be everlasting, and may his spirit continue to inspire us all."

Indeed, Nathaniel's legacy extends far beyond his tragic fall. He represents the best of what it means to be a lone soldier - the courage to leave behind the familiar, the determination to serve a cause greater than oneself, and the capacity to find joy and purpose in that service.

The stories of Rose Lubin, Ilan Cohen, and Nathaniel Young exemplify a profound form of heroism that goes beyond battlefield bravery. These young individuals, barely out of their teens, made choices that set them apart from their peers. While many of their contemporaries were focused on college applications or planning gap year adventures, these lone soldiers chose a path of service and sacrifice. Their decision to leave the comfort and safety of their homes to defend a country they loved, even if they weren't born there, demonstrates maturity far beyond their years. When we read these stories, we are reminded that true heroism often begins with a choice to grow up faster, take on responsibilities, and live for something greater than oneself.

CHAPTER FOUR

HEROIC BROTHERHOOD: HEROES FROM THE BEDOUIN COMMUNITY

*"Behold, how good and how pleasant it is
for brethren to dwell together in unity!"*
Psalm 133:1

"Our conscience wouldn't allow us to leave them there, under fire. Before we went to evacuate our cousin, we helped many other people who were at the party... we evacuated at least 30-40 people who were at the party."
–Ismail Alqrinawi

The slaughter of October 7 was an attack on the Jewish people and the vast majority of victims were Jewish men, women and children. However, it is important to remember that many other people were also impacted by the horrific Hamas attack, including Christians, Muslims, Druze, and Bedouins.

Alongside the Jewish heroes of October 7, four

Bedouin men from Rahat exemplified extraordinary humanity and compassion, heroically risking their lives to save others. The story of Ismail Alqrinawi and his cousins demonstrates how human decency and dignity transcend any cultural differences.

Early on that fateful Saturday morning, Ismail Alqrinawi and three of his cousins set out from their home in Rahat with the goal of rescuing their relative Hisham, who worked at Kibbutz Be'eri. Rahat, the largest Bedouin city in Israel, is located in the Negev desert, about 30 kilometers from the Gaza Strip. But what began as a family rescue mission quickly transformed into a much larger humanitarian effort as the scale of the Hamas attacks became apparent. Hamas terrorists initiated a massive, coordinated assault on multiple locations in southern Israel catching IDF forces off guard and creating a chaotic and terrifying situation for civilians in the area.

As Ismail and his cousins made their way towards Be'eri, the four men encountered a scene of chaos and carnage near Kibbutz Re'im, where the Supernova music festival was under attack. The festival, an all-night electronic music event, had drawn thousands of young people from across Israel. As dawn broke, it became the site of one of the worst massacres in Israeli history. Terrorists indiscriminately murdered 364 people at the festival and took dozens more as hostages. Confronted with the sight of terrified civilians fleeing for their lives, the Alqrinawi cousins made a critical choice. They could not simply pass by without offering aid. As Ismail recounted, "Our conscience wouldn't allow us to leave them there, under fire." This decisive action not only demonstrated their profound humanity but also saved dozens of lives amid the chaos.

The four men began loading panicked festival-goers into their vehicle, ferrying them to safety before returning to rescue more. They estimate rescuing between 30-40 people from the area around the festival site. With each group they evacuated, the cousins showed remarkable compassion - hugging the traumatized survivors, giving them water, and helping them contact loved ones. Amid chaos and violence, these simple acts of kindness comforted people who had just experienced unimaginable horror.

Their actions stand in stark contrast to the brutality unfolding around them. As Ismail described the horrific scenes he witnessed - piles of bodies, widespread brutality - it's clear the psychological toll was immense. "I remember the dead bodies I saw on the road, the dead bodies I saw in the fields. That is something that you cannot forget," he said, tears in his eyes. Yet the men persevered, driven by an ethical imperative to help their fellow human beings regardless of background.

After spending hours rescuing festival attendees, the cousins pressed on toward their original destination of Be'eri to find Hisham. By this point, they understood they were driving into an active war zone, with gunfire and explosions all around them.

Kibbutz Be'eri, like many communities near the Gaza border, was under severe attack. Hamas terrorists had infiltrated the kibbutz, going from house to house and butchering civilians, including children. The situation was dire, with many residents trapped in safe rooms or hiding wherever they could.

Near Be'eri, they managed to locate and rescue not only Hisham but also Aya Meydan, a local resident who had been hiding in the bushes for hours. Meydan's account provides a harrowing glimpse into the terror gripping the kibbutz, as residents desperately sought shelter from roving bands of heavily armed terrorists.

Meydan, an avid cyclist, had left early that morning for a bike ride. She had barely exited the kibbutz gates when the rocket barrage began, forcing her to take cover. On her way back, she encountered Hisham, who warned her of the terrorists inside the kibbutz. Together, they fled and hid in thorny bushes, witnessing unspeakable violence around them.

For hours, Meydan and Hisham lay hidden, hearing constant gunfire and explosions. The arrival of Ismail and his cousins quite literally meant the difference between life and death. The rescue was not without further peril, as the group was stopped by IDF soldiers who initially mistook them for terrorists.

Even after safely evacuating Meydan and Hisham, the cousins' sense of duty did not end. When Meydan was placed on an evacuation bus to Beersheba, they followed alongside to ensure her continued safety.

Ismail Alqrinawi and his cousins, like many non-Jewish citizens of Israel, demonstrate a deep love for their country and its diverse populace, challenging simplistic narratives about the Israeli-Arab conflict. As Bedouin citizens of Israel, and their heroism on October 7 demonstrates that in moments of crisis, our shared humanity can transcend ethnic and religious divisions.

Israel's Bedouin community, numbering around 270,000, has a unique position in Israeli society. While they are citizens of Israel, they are also considered Arab nomads, and live on the fringe of both the Arab and Israeli communities. However, many Bedouins also serve in the Israel Defense Forces, particularly in tracking and desert warfare units where their traditional skills are highly valued. The actions of the Alqrinawi cousins highlight the mutual respect between the Bedouin community and broader Israeli society.

Their story is part of a larger pattern of Arab Israelis who stepped up to help their fellow citizens during and after the attacks. From Bedouin search and rescue teams to Arab business owners donating supplies, these acts of solidarity reveal the potential for coexistence and mutual support between Israel's diverse communities.

Bedouin tribes in the Negev desert were especially quick to mobilize volunteer teams to assist in the search for missing Israelis. Sleman Shlebe, from the Bedouin town of Bir Hadaj, told the Israeli newspaper *Haaretz*, "We heard about people missing from both the Arab and Jewish communities, and knew that thanks to our exceptional familiarity with the south we could help."

In another touching example, Arab-Israeli business owner Alaa Amara donated some 50 children's bicycles to families evacuated from communities around Gaza to the majority-Jewish town of Tzur Yitzhak. "I did it to benefit the children," he told *The Times of Israel*. "They don't know about war."

The bravery of the Alqrinawi cousins has rightfully been celebrated, including recognition from Israeli police officials. Brigadier General Efi Shayman's meeting with the family and his words - "Bedouins are our brothers" - speak to the unifying power of their actions. As Ismail himself stated, "As Jews and Arabs, we are partners, citizens, and we give our contribution to the nation."

This sentiment was echoed by other prominent Arab-Israeli voices in the aftermath of October 7. Lucy Aharish, an Arab-Israeli news anchor, declared her support for Israel in a televised newscast that went viral. "Since Saturday morning, the State of Israel is under attack. Our beloved country is under attack," she said, emphasizing the shared citizenship and common cause of all Israelis in the face of terror.

The story of the four Bedouin brothers from Rahat is ultimately one of hope. It reminds us that even in the face of heinous acts of terror and hatred, there are individuals willing to risk everything to save the lives of others. Their actions embody the highest ideals of human compassion and courage.

On October 7, 2023, Ismail Alqrinawi and his cousins chose compassion, bravery, and selflessness. Their story is not just one of individual heroism but a powerful example of the potential for unity and shared purpose in Israeli society.

CHAPTER FIVE

HEROIC LEADER: ANER SHAPIRA

"I charge you: Be strong and resolute;
do not be terrified or dismayed, for the ETERNAL
your God is with you wherever you go."
Joshua 1:9

> "Guys, don't worry!" he called out.
> "I'm a soldier, my comrades are nearby, I'm here.
> Everything will be all right!"

Aner Elyakim Shapira was born and raised in the heart of Jerusalem. The eldest of seven children born to Shira and Moshe Shapira, Aner grew up with a deep connection to his birthplace. Jerusalem, with its rich tapestry of cultures and religions, became a wellspring of inspiration for the budding artist and musician.

From a young age, Aner displayed a remarkable blend of creativity and introspection. His mother, Shira, recalls, "Aner's connection to Jerusalem was very deep. He loved music, he loved art, and he loved Jerusalem. Many of his songs are about Jerusalem. He was exploring the unique atmosphere of the city: Jews, Arabs, orthodox, secular, religious, the mix in Jerusalem, the vibe of the street."

This deep-rooted love for his city would shape Aner's artistic journey and philosophical outlook throughout his life. He was particularly drawn to the Ben Sira bar in Jerusalem, which his mother described as having "a unique atmosphere... It's people who love peace, love music, care about justice. Very special people." This environment nurtured Aner's growing passion for music and art, as well as his developing worldview.

Aner's artistic journey began early. As a child, he played piano and developed an appreciation for classical music. However, it was in his teenage years that Aner found his true artistic voice. He became enamored with hip-hop and rap, genres that allowed him to express his thoughts and observations about the world around him. This transition from classical to contemporary forms of music reflected Aner's evolving artistic sensibilities and his desire to engage with current social and political issues through his art.

His creative process was profoundly personal. According to his family, Aner aimed to "capture his inner world and place the end of a thread on a page." The connection between the melodies and texts he created was natural, resulting in the composition of dozens of songs. This description reveals Aner's artistic method—an introspective approach focused on translating his inner experiences and observations into tangible artistic forms.

Aner's notebook reflected his multifaceted artistic talents. It was filled with sketches, ranging from views of Jerusalem to surreal faces. This blend of realistic depictions of his beloved city with more abstract, surreal elements showcases the depth and range of Aner's artistic vision. His ability to move between different styles and forms of expression demonstrates a versatility that is rare in an artist so young.

As Aner's artistic skills developed, so too did the themes and subjects of his work. His music touched on themes of social justice, peace, and the human condition - topics that reflected his growing awareness of the world around him and his desire to engage with important social and political issues through his art. This engagement with weighty themes demonstrates Aner's maturity and his commitment to using his art as a means of commentary and, potentially, a catalyst for change.

One of Aner's songs, written three years before the events that would claim his life, eerily foreshadowed the conflict to come. It spoke of children in the south of Israel sitting in bomb shelters, rockets in the sky, fear, and death. It serves as a chilling reminder of the persistent threat of terror that Israeli citizens face daily and the profound impact it has on the lives of ordinary people.

Another song, composed during the 2023 political protests in Israel, addresses the issue of brotherly hatred, calling for unity and understanding among his fellow citizens. Aner's debut selection of songs, titled "Introduction to Anarchism," contained six songs that he wrote, composed, and produced. These songs, as his family explained, "talk about the pre-war situation as a prophecy of rage for these days, as a point of light for the future." The title of the Extended Play ("EP") and the description of its content provide insight into Aner's political and social views. The reference to anarchism suggests a critique of existing power structures, while the description of the songs as both a "prophecy of rage" and a "point of light for the future" indicates a nuanced view that acknowledges current problems while maintaining hope for positive change.

Aner's dream was to release an album of his songs, but like many young artists, he faced financial constraints. Undeterred, he planned to produce a collection of merchandise featuring his art - T-shirts, bags, and hats - to raise funds for his musical endeavors. While Aner was passionate about his artistic pursuits, he also felt a strong sense of duty to his country. After high school, he attended an army preparatory program for candidates for elite IDF units.

Aner's path to military service was not without obstacles. During the field exercises that determine unit assignments, Aner was injured and required surgery. This setback could have deterred many, but Aner's determination shone through. He used his recovery time productively, setting up a home studio where he continued to write and record music. This period of forced inactivity became a time of intense creativity, further developing his musical skills and expanding his repertoire.

A second attempt to join an elite army unit also resulted in injury, and Aner had to wait 15 months before he could begin his service. This extended period of waiting and recovery tested Aner's resolve, but he remained committed to his goal of serving in an elite unit. During this time, he continued to focus on his music, using the challenges he faced as inspiration for his art.

Finally, Aner achieved his goal of joining the Nahal Brigade, an infantry unit known for combining military service with volunteer work. This unique combination of military duty and community service aligned well with Aner's values and his desire to make a positive impact on society.

Aner's decision to serve in the military might seem at odds with his artistic, peace-loving nature. However, his mother Shira explains the apparent contradiction: "Aner believed in taking a stand. He believed very deeply in the good of people, in the importance of making peace and trying to talk to each other rather than fighting each other. He believed that human nature is good and that if you don't put people into a regime of power, they will do good."

"It sounds like a contradiction, but for Aner, it wasn't. He believed that in an ideal world, you don't need the army. But as long as we have the army and we need to defend ourselves, he must do his best to defend people. This is the combination that worked for him."

This philosophy - of standing up for what's right while still believing in the fundamental goodness of humanity - would ultimately define Aner's final, heroic act. It speaks to a nuanced worldview that recognizes the complexities of the situation in Israel while maintaining a fundamental optimism about human nature and the possibility of peace.

On October 7, 2023, Aner Shapira's life took an unexpected and tragic turn. After celebrating Simchat Torah with his family, the 22-year-old soldier, on leave from his duties with the Nahal Brigade, decided to attend the Nova music festival at Kibbutz Reim with his best friend, Hersh Goldberg-Polin. As a full-time soldier, he missed the music scene and planned to take advantage of his short time off.

When Hamas terrorists launched their surprise attack on southern Israel, Aner and Hersh, along with other festival-goers, found themselves in a desperate situation. The joyous atmosphere of the festival was shattered, replaced by chaos and fear as missiles began to fall and gunfire erupted.

Seeking shelter, Aner and Hersh ran to a small roadside bomb shelter near the Re'im intersection. Inside, they found about 30 young men and women already squeezed into the tiny space, trying to escape the bombing. The shelter was packed with people. The air was incredibly tense. Everyone inside was gripped by fear and uncertainty about their situation.

It was in this moment of crisis that Aner's true character shone through. Survivors recall that when Aner saw the panic in people's eyes, he immediately took charge and tried to calm everyone down. "Guys, don't worry!" he called out. "I'm a soldier, my comrades are nearby, I'm here. Everything will be all right!"

This instinctive move to reassure and lead others

in a moment of extreme danger speaks volumes about Aner's character. Despite being off-duty and in a situation more perilous than any he had faced in his military service, Aner stepped up, drawing on his training and natural leadership abilities to provide a sense of calm and direction to those around him.

As the sound of gunfire drew closer, Aner realized that the terrorists were about to throw grenades into the shelter. At that moment, he made a decision that would save many lives and tragically cost him his own. Turning to his impromptu team, he said, "I'm going to catch the grenades and throw them back. Watch me! If anything happens to me, take over and continue what I am doing."

What followed was an extraordinary display of courage and quick thinking. Aner managed to catch and throw back seven grenades in total, each time risking his life to protect those around him. His actions saved numerous lives and bought precious time for the people in the shelter.

The physical and mental strength required for such an act is almost unimaginable. Each time Aner caught a grenade, he was literally holding death in his hands, with only seconds to react and throw it back out of the shelter. The stress and fear in those moments must have been overwhelming, yet Aner persevered, driven by his desire to protect others.

Dashcam footage from that day captured Aner's heroic actions. The video shows him standing at the entrance of the shelter, catching and throwing back grenades hurled by the terrorists. Tragically, it was the eighth grenade that proved fatal. The explosive detonated in Aner's hand, mortally wounding him.

In the aftermath of the attack, survivors shared their accounts of Aner's bravery. Agam Yosefzon, one of those in the shelter, remembered, "What I remember about him is that straight away, he said there was a terrorist intrusion and gave us certainty, and even though he didn't say much he made us feel calm. I remember saying to him, 'Thank you for coming here, you're keeping us calm.' That was the last thing I remember saying to him before everything happened."

She added, "He had this sense of quiet about him. I've never seen so much nobility in one person." The firsthand accounts from that day provide a vivid picture of Aner's demeanor in those crucial moments - calm, reassuring, and noble in his sacrifice.

Another survivor, Itamar Shapira (no relation to Aner), presented Aner's parents with two photos he had taken inside the shelter. The photos show Aner standing at the entrance while others crouch behind him, providing a visual testament to his protective stance. Itamar described Aner's actions: "He spotted the grenade straight away and threw it out quickly, in less than three seconds. What's extraordinary is that you don't know how long they were holding it before they threw it inside. It's the most courageous thing I've ever seen anyone do in my life. He's a hero."

News of Aner's heroic sacrifice spread quickly, touching hearts across Israel and around the world.

His story soon became a symbol of Israeli courage and selflessness in the face of terror.

For Aner's family and friends, the loss was devastating. Yet, in their grief, they found purpose in ensuring that Aner's memory and his art would live on. They resolved to fulfill his dream of releasing his music to the world.

After Aner's death, his family and friends began the painstaking process of going through his recordings. They discovered about 60 projects, of which 30 songs were complete enough to be released. This treasure trove of music became the foundation for posthumously fulfilling Aner's artistic vision.

The family released an album titled "Anerchism," featuring six of Aner's songs. Five of these were composed and produced by Aner himself before his death. The sixth song, "Hatred of Brothers," was completed with the help of rapper and producer Avery G., and features a final verse written and recorded by Shaanan Streett of the popular Israeli hip-hop group Hadag Nachash.

The music video for "Hatred of Brothers" was filmed in Jerusalem, featuring Aner's friends and family in the city he loved so dearly. It includes brief glimpses of Aner himself, along with shots of his parents, siblings, and friends in the local haunts where he spent time. The video ends poignantly with Shaanan Streett rapping the final verse in a small downtown bar, symbolically saving seats for both Aner and his friend Hersh, who was taken hostage by Hamas terrorists on October 7 and, at the time of writing, remains in captivity.

This collaborative effort to complete and release

Aner's music serves multiple purposes. It fulfills Aner's dream of sharing his art with the world, provides a means for his family and friends to process their grief, and creates a lasting memorial to Aner's talent and vision. The involvement of established artists like Shaanan Streett also helps to bring Aner's music to a wider audience, ensuring his voice continues to be heard.

Aner's artwork has also found new life and appreciation. His sketches and designs have been shared widely, with graphic artists creating new works inspired by Aner's style. One notable extension of his music was shared by The Israeli Symphonic Orchestra. One of Aner's songs was adapted and performed in a classical music concert. The impact of Aner's story reached far beyond Israel's borders. In southern France, a city dedicated a square to Aner's memory, a testament to how his courage resonated with people around the world.

While Aner's music and art form a significant part of his legacy, his parents, Shira and Moshe Shapira, emphasize that his heroic and ethical legacy is equally important. They see his final actions as a conscious choice to do good until the very last moment of his life.

Shira Shapira reflects on this, saying, "It's a very special message that he left us, that you can choose, until the very last minute of your life, to do good. It's in your hands! Literally, it was in his hands when he used his hands to throw the grenades back." This powerful statement encapsulates the essence of Aner's legacy - the idea that we always have a choice to act with courage and compassion, even in the most dire circumstances.

Another crucial aspect of Aner's legacy, according to his mother, is the importance of taking a stand. "It's something we can learn from his songs and his attitude towards life. You don't sit and wait for things to happen. You take a stand." This ethos of active engagement with life and its challenges is reflected in both Aner's art and his final heroic act.

The Shapira family has found comfort in connecting with the survivors of the attack, those whose lives Aner saved through his actions. Many of these survivors attended Aner's funeral and have since formed close bonds with his family. Shira Shapira says, "What brings comfort is that he saved so many people and gave them life. We won't get to see him have children, but we were privileged to see those whom he saved, who will go on to have children and will live good and happy lives."

Today, Aner's name and memory live on throughout Jerusalem. His distinctive signature - just three letters in Hebrew, the "*ayin*" hugging a smaller "*nun*" and "*resh*" in a thick, black scrawl - can be seen graffitied on walls, on white stickers stuck to telephone poles, and scrawled on boards throughout the city. It's a constant reminder of a young man who loved his city deeply and gave his life to protect others.

This grassroots memorialization of Aner speaks to the deep impact his story has had on his community. The proliferation of his signature throughout Jerusalem transforms the city itself into a kind of living memorial, with each instance serving as a reminder of Aner's life, art, and sacrifice.

In the words of his mother, "We see his whole life, not just what's being spoken about now — that's just the tip of the iceberg. He had a whole life, which ended too soon, in which he was an amazing friend, son, brother and grandson, who always treated people in the best possible way."

Aner Elyakim Shapira's life was cut tragically short at the age of 22, but in that brief time, he touched countless lives through his art, his music, his friendship, and, ultimately, his sacrifice. His story is one of creativity, courage, and unwavering commitment to doing what's right, even in the face of unimaginable danger.

CHAPTER SIX

HEROIC FIRST RESPONDERS: ANSWERING THE CALL OF DUTY

But Rut replied, "Do not urge me to leave you,
to turn back and not follow you. For wherever you go,
I will go; wherever you lodge, I will lodge; your people
shall be my people, and your God my God."
Ruth 1:6

"They're here. They're in the clinic.
I don't think I'll make it out of here. I love you."
–Amit Mann

AMIT MANN: A HEROINE UNTIL THE VERY END

Born and raised in Kibbutz Be'eri, 22-year-old Amit had always been drawn to the medical field. Her journey began in 2015 when she joined Magen David Adom (MDA), Israel's national emergency medical service, as a youth volunteer. From the outset, Amit's natural aptitude for medical care and her unwavering dedication quickly set her apart. Her early experiences with MDA weren't just formative; they solidified her resolve to pursue a career in medicine.

As Amit advanced from a volunteer to an Emergency Medical Technician (EMT) and then to a paramedic, her dedication to saving lives only deepened. With every role she took on, her drive for knowledge and commitment to excellence became more evident. Her colleagues recall her as a steady presence amidst the chaos of emergencies, with her meticulous care for patients defining her professionalism. It was only natural that she soon became a teacher. She completed a course for instructors and began training new volunteers, sharing her knowledge and enthusiasm with the next generation of emergency responders.

Just two months before October 7, Amit began teaching the regional paramedic course in the Negev. This new role was a testament to her expertise and the trust placed in her by MDA. As an instructor, Amit didn't just impart knowledge; she instilled in her students the same sense of duty and compassion that drove her. Her dream was to study medicine and continue saving lives on a larger scale, a dream that, tragically, she would not live to fulfill.

On the morning of October 7, Kibbutz Be'eri, Amit's home and workplace, became a battleground. The clinic where Amit was treating the wounded from the initial barrage soon found itself under siege.

For six grueling hours, Amit was trapped in the clinic, surrounded by the injured and the fallen. The terrorists' attempts to breach the facility were relentless, yet Amit's focus remained unshakeable. In these dire circumstances, her true character shone through. Despite the imminent danger to her own life, Amit continued to provide medical care, her patients' well-being her sole priority.

Through WhatsApp messages to her sisters, Amit painted a heart-wrenching picture of the unfolding tragedy. "There's a nurse and a dentist here. We're doing what we can. Many injured people are bleeding out, but there is no way to evacuate them."

As the siege wore on, Amit's messages to her sister Lior took on a more urgent tone. "I don't think I'll make it out of here. Please be strong if something happens to me," she texted, her courage evident even in the face of her own mortality.

Tragically, the terrorists eventually breached the clinic. Amit's final words: "They're on me! They shot my legs!" were her last act of defiance against the terrorists. When the dust settled, Amit's body was found among at least 107 others in Kibbutz Be'eri.

The news of Amit Mann's death reverberated through her community and across Israel. She was remembered not just for her final act of heroism, but for a life dedicated to helping others. Magen David Adom Director General Eli Bin eulogized her as a "heroic paramedic who prioritized her patients' lives even in the face of extreme danger."

Amit's best friend and fellow paramedic, Oshrit Haddad, offered a poignant tribute: "Amit was always there for everyone... On Saturday, while terrorists were shooting at them, she continued to help patients and tried to save their lives. She fought for their lives until the last moments." In the aftermath of the October 7 attack,

Amit's story became a rallying point for her community and the nation at large. It served as a poignant reminder of the human cost of terrorism and the indomitable spirit of those who dedicate their lives to saving others. Amit's sacrifice showed just how vital a role that first responders play in times of crisis - and the dangers they often face in carrying out their duties.

Amit Mann's legacy challenges us all to live up to her example – to face danger with courage, to serve others selflessly, and to never lose sight of our shared humanity, even in the darkest hours. Her story, though tragically cut short, continues to inspire and remind us of the profound impact one individual can have on the world around them.

ZAKA: HEROES AMIDST THE DARKNESS

In the days that followed Hamas' brutal attack on October 7, a group of extraordinary volunteers were called upon to confront the unthinkable. These are the members of ZAKA, Israel's premier search and rescue organization, and this is their story of unwavering courage in the face of unspeakable horror.

ZAKA, which stands for Zihuy Korbanot Ason (Disaster Victim Identification), emerged out of necessity in the late 1980s. What began as a small group of "crazy people," as founding member Yossi Landau described them, soon grew into an internationally recognized symbol of hope, with thousands of volunteers across Israel and around the world.

At the heart of ZAKA's mission lies a sacred duality:

to preserve life when possible and when that proves impossible, to ensure dignity in death. This purpose is rooted in the profound Jewish belief in the sanctity of human life and the importance of proper burial. ZAKA volunteers, trained as emergency medical technicians, stand ready to respond to accidents and attacks with the goal of saving lives. Yet when faced with the grim reality of death, they transform into guardians of the deceased, meticulously collecting every trace of human remains to ensure a proper Jewish burial.

On a typical day, these yellow-vested sentinels are at the scenes of life's everyday tragedies—car accidents, fires, isolated acts of violence, and, in the reality of daily life in Israel, the aftermath of terrorist attacks. Yet, nothing in their extensive experience could have prepared them for the horrors that unfolded on October 7.

As most Israelis celebrated Simchat Torah, still blessedly ignorant of the horrific attack on southern Israel, ZAKA volunteer Simcha Greiniman received a call that would forever change his life. By 2:20 PM, a bus filled with volunteers from Modiin Illit in central Israel was hurtling south, its occupants unaware of the Dantean landscape that awaited them.

As they approached Sderot, the volunteers saw devastation that defied comprehension. Overturned and charred vehicles littered the highway, grim markers of lives brutally interrupted. Though they wanted to stop and begin their sacred work, the IDF warned that terrorists were still in the area and the rescuers themselves had become potential prey.

In Sderot, they encountered a nightmarish scene. A somber mountain of 22 bodies greeted them, with more arriving by the minute. Faced with an impossible equation - the need for dignified handling versus the very real danger of bodies being taken into Gaza - the ZAKA team made the heart-wrenching decision to prioritize recovery over protocol.

As they worked, the sounds of terror provided a grim soundtrack. Gunfire erupting from the nearby police station and the steady sound of rockets forced the volunteers to regularly seek cover. Yet they persevered, driven by their sacred mission and the knowledge that every body recovered was a family spared further anguish.

The horrors deepened as they traversed Highway 34. Every vehicle they encountered told a silent story of unimaginable brutality. Open doors and trails of blood spoke of desperate attempts to flee. Finding two bullet-riddled child car seats shook even the toughest among them with a wave of grief. Another vehicle, so thoroughly consumed by flames that its occupants were reduced to ash, required specialized equipment to gather what remained.

By the end of that hellish day, Greiniman and his team had collected 72 bodies – a grim mosaic of police officers, soldiers, civilians, and terrorists. Their truck, designed for equipment transport, bore a cargo of sorrow, filled floor to ceiling with the victims of this unprecedented attack. But their work was far from over.

For 18 relentless days, ZAKA volunteers moved through the devastated communities of southern Israel like angels of mercy in a hell on earth. They processed 1,750 vehicles containing human remains, ensuring that every drop of blood and every fragment of bone, was collected for proper burial.

The emotional toll on these volunteers is beyond measure. Simcha Greiniman speaks of knowing "what happened in every house" while deliberately avoiding learning the victims' names - a psychological shield that allows him to continue his vital work. Yet even with this self-imposed distance, the burden of their experiences is one these heroes will carry for the rest of their lives.

In the aftermath of October 7, ZAKA volunteers have taken on an additional mantle: witnesses to history. They have stood before the United Nations, met with members of the U.S. Congress, and addressed parliaments across Europe. Their firsthand accounts and meticulous documentation serve as a bulwark against those who would deny or minimize the atrocities committed by Hamas.

What compels individuals to volunteer for such harrowing work? For many ZAKA members, it is a profound sense of mission, a duty to their fellow humans that transcends the boundaries of faith and nationality. Greiniman expresses it simply: "My life has a mission – I am here for the Jewish people. It is a merit to help families recover the bodies of their loved ones and help them to reach closure. I am doing something that not everyone is able to do."

This sense of purpose allows ZAKA volunteers to push through the trauma and continue their sacred work. Like firefighters who run towards danger while others flee, ZAKA members willingly enter scenes of unspeakable horror to fulfill their mission of mercy and provide dignity even in the most undignified of situations.

The heroism of ZAKA is not limited to its Jewish volunteers. The organization includes members from all of Israel's diverse communities, including Arab Israelis like Jamal Waraqi. Speaking of his experiences on October 7, Waraqi emphasized the shared humanity that transcends religious and ethnic divides: "We are in a situation together with Jews, Muslims, Christians, Druze. It's impossible to differentiate. The State of Israel is one body, we are the left hand, the Jews are the right, and a body can't work if one of the hands doesn't work. We have to be one body, one soul."

As Israel and the world continue to grapple with the aftermath of that terrible day, the men and women of ZAKA remain steadfast in their mission. They are the keepers of memory, the guardians of dignity, and the living embodiment of hope in humanity's darkest hours. In their unwavering commitment to honor the dead and comfort the living, they remind us all of the extraordinary heights the human spirit can reach, even when confronted with the depths of human cruelty.

THE BATTLE OF SDEROT POLICE STATION: HEROISM IN THE FACE OF TERROR

With a population of over 33,000, Sderot is the largest Israeli town on the Gaza border - and historically the most frequent target of Hamas rockets and terror attacks. On October 7, the city once again became a target, as Hamas terrorists invaded. In the hours that followed the attack, a group of police officers were called upon to confront the unthinkable.

As rockets pierced the morning sky and Hamas terrorists breached the nearby border, Sderot, nestled less than a mile from Gaza, found itself at the epicenter of Hamas's brutal assault. While most residents sought shelter, the officers of the Sderot police station steeled themselves for the fight of their lives. The air raid sirens that had become all too familiar to the residents of this border town now heralded a threat far greater than any they had faced before.

Commander Sgt. Maj. Adir Shlomo, the 47-year-old head of logistics, rushed to the station from his adjacent home, telling his wife with grim prescience, "I think I'm the last one to go." His words would prove tragically prophetic. Within moments of arrival, he became one of the first to fall as terrorists stormed the building, his sacrifice marking the beginning of a long and bloody struggle.

The Sderot police station quickly became a primary target for the invading forces. A fierce, hours-long battle ensued as a handful of officers fought desperately against waves of heavily armed attackers. The disparity in numbers was stark, but the defenders' resolve was unshakeable.

Superintendent Shoshana Mali, the duty officer on that fateful morning, found herself thrust into the role of battlefield commander. Leading a valiant defense from the rooftop alongside six comrades, Mali embodied the spirit of resistance that would define the day. As bullets tore through the air and comrades fell around her, Mali, though wounded, fought on. Her leadership in those crucial early hours would prove instrumental in rallying the defenders and organizing their resistance.

Inside, the station became a maze of life-and-death struggles. Officers engaged in room-to-room combat. The walls, soon riddled with bullet holes, bore silent witness to their courage. Every corridor became a battleground, every office a potential stronghold. The defenders used their intimate knowledge of the building's layout to their advantage, setting up ambushes and creating chokepoints to slow the terrorists' advance.

The battle was not confined to the station alone. Beyond its walls, other heroes emerged in the streets of Sderot. Elor Tawil, a volunteer with Magen David Adom, Israel's emergency medical service, exemplified the courage of first responders that day. Despite the obvious dangers, Tawil and his colleagues chose to run towards the sound of gunfire rather than away from it.

Tawil braved gunfire-swept streets in an armored ambulance, a thin shell of protection against the onslaught around him. He and his fellow paramedics raced to evacuate the wounded. Their actions saved countless lives.

For hours, the defenders of the Sderot police station held their ground. Though vastly outnumbered and outgunned, they refused to yield. Their stand prevented the terrorists from capturing this strategic location, likely saving hundreds of civilian lives in Sderot and beyond.

The cost of this victory was steep. The brave officers, including Adir Shlomo, gave their lives to defend their community. Shlomo, remembered by colleagues as the "soul of the station," epitomized the selfless dedication of these fallen heroes. His loss was felt keenly by all who knew him, a reminder of the human cost of courage.

Their sacrifice was not in vain. By tying up large numbers of terrorists for hours, they bought precious time for civilians to reach safety and for military reinforcements to arrive. In those crucial early hours, when the fate of Sderot hung in the balance, it was the determination of these few officers that made the difference between life and death for the people of Sderot.

The battle for the Sderot police station quickly became a powerful symbol of resistance, not just for the city but for all of Israel. Even as the fighting raged and the building crumbled under the assault, the sight of the Israeli flag still flying over the beleaguered station sent a message of unyielding determination.

In the hours following the attack, the Israeli army destroyed the Police Station. After determining that all of the remaining Israeli officers had been rescued, they detonated the station to make sure that the terrorists from that battle would never be able to wreak havoc again. The ruined station stood as a somber memorial to the events of October 7. Its rubble, marked by a lone Israeli flag and memorial candles, became a pilgrimage site for those seeking to pay their respects. Each shattered wall and bullet-scarred surface told a story of courage under fire, a physical reminder of the price of freedom.

Israeli Prime Minister Benjamin Netanyahu, visiting the site weeks later, captured the nation's sentiment as he saluted the survivors: "On behalf of the entire people of Israel and all citizens of Israel, I salute you; you are genuine heroes." He spoke for the entire nation of Israel. Plans to rebuild the station quickly took shape, both as a practical necessity and as a symbol of resilience. Netanyahu vowed, "The police [station] behind us was demolished and we are building a new one, but this attests to what happened here." The commitment to rebuild was more than just about replacing a building; it was a statement of defiance, a promise that terror would not have the final word.

On a human level, the battle juxtaposes the depths of cruelty with the heights of heroism. The barbarism of the terrorists stands in stark relief against the selfless courage of the first responders who risked everything to save others. It serves as a reminder of the ongoing threats faced by Israel but also of the incredible bravery and resilience of its people when faced with existential danger. In their honor, and in honor of Amit Mann and the Zaka officers, we must strive to build a future worthy of their sacrifice, one where peace and security are not just aspirations but realities.

CHAPTER SEVEN

HEROIC HEALING: THE UNBREAKABLE BODY AND MIND OF THE VICTIMS OF OCTOBER 7

Hashem, my God, I cried out to You, and You healed me.
(Psalm 30:2)

"If we were both destined to lose a limb, it's best that we both experienced the same thing," –Gali Segal

The October 7 Hamas attacks and the subsequent war in Gaza have left thousands of Israelis physically and emotionally wounded. Among the injured were civilians caught in the initial onslaught and soldiers who fought to defend their country. This chapter examines three remarkable stories of recovery - the journey of Gali Segal and Ben Binyamin, a young couple both gravely wounded at the Supernova music festival; Shlomo Klein, a soldier injured defending his base; and Mia Schem, a civilian taken hostage and later released in the first Hostage release deal in late 2023. Their experiences of trauma, resilience, and healing offer powerful insights into the long road of recovery faced by many Israelis in the wake of October 7.

LOVE CONQUERS ALL: GALI SEGAL AND BEN BINYAMIN

The story of Gali Segal and Ben Binyamin is one of love triumphing over unimaginable pain.

The couple, who had been dating for seven years, got engaged during a trip to Italy, where Ben proposed with a ring and a bouquet of roses. Gali was studying interior design, and Ben was working in real estate while also playing soccer in the Israeli national league as a defender.

On October 6th, they attended the Supernova music festival near Kibbutz Re'im to celebrate their future together. But instead of a joyful celebration, they found themselves fighting for their lives when Hamas terrorists attacked early the next morning, killing hundreds and taking dozens hostage. As the first rockets hit, Gali, Ben, and a friend tried to escape by car, but their tires were shot out by terrorists. Trapped, they sought refuge in a roadside bomb shelter near the Alumim Junction, together with others seeking safety.

Their relief was short-lived. Terrorists soon arrived and began firing at the shelter. A grenade was thrown into the crowded space, and the explosion knocked both Gali and Ben unconscious. When they regained consciousness, they were horrified to find that they had both lost their right legs above the knee. Gali remembers seeing a friend walk out of the shelter, unsure whether to stay or flee, while she and Ben could not call out for help.

Gali recalled, "I went into complete shock. I screamed, 'I don't have a leg!' And Ben, next to me, said, 'Save your strength! Stop screaming!' He said to me, 'If that's our fate, if that's what's supposed to happen to us, at least we're together.' It felt like the end."

Amid the chaos, a SWAT officer arrived, exchanging fire with the terrorists and managing to get inside the shelter to help the wounded. Thanks to his actions, Gali and Ben survived. They were pulled from the shelter and taken to ambulances, but neither knew if the other was still alive.

Gali describes the shock and fear she felt in the ambulance and at the hospital, where she kept asking for Ben. When they finally saw each other in the hospital, they were overwhelmed with relief to know they were both alive, despite the devastating loss of their legs.

Their parallel injuries, while tragic, became a source of strength. "If we were both destined to lose a limb, it's best that we both experienced the same thing," Gali shared. Ben added, "There's a huge advantage in going through this together, experiencing the exact same process. It's immensely comforting for me on an emotional level."

The couple's journey of recovery has been long and challenging. Gali has undergone seven surgeries, while Ben has had three. Beyond the physical toll, they've had to grapple with the emotional trauma of the attack and the loss of their friend Shani Gabbay, who was killed at the festival.

Yet through it all, Gali and Ben have found strength in each other and in their love. Their determination to move forward together has been a source of strength not just for them, but for many Israelis grappling with the aftermath of October 7.

Their resilience is best exemplified by their unwavering commitment to their planned wedding. Despite the enormous challenges they faced, Gali and Ben remained determined to walk down the aisle together. "We want to go to the wedding with a prosthesis, walking," Gali had said. Ben added with a smile, "She already knows what prosthesis she wants and everything."

On July 25, 2024, their dream became a reality. After months of intensive rehabilitation and unwavering determination, Gali and Ben celebrated their wedding, marking a triumphant milestone in their journey of recovery and love. True to her wish, Gali adorned her prosthetic leg with white glitter, especially for the occasion.

The wedding was a testament to the couple's resilience and the support they received. The entire medical staff who had cared for them during their long months of rehabilitation attended the celebration. Dr. Mickey Dudkiewicz, director of Hillel Yaffe Medical Center, remarked that it was "the first time I've come to the wedding of patients. From the meeting at the trauma room, at the time of greatest difficulty, to this place that symbolizes happiness and a continuation."

Singer Shlomi Shabat, who had met the couple during their hospital stay, kept his promise to perform at their wedding, adding to the joyous atmosphere.

Ben, who was a professional soccer player in the Israeli second division before the injury, now plays for the Israeli national amputee soccer team. This new passion has become part of his journey of recovery and adaptation.

Gali's mother, Orly, captured the significance of the moment, saying, "They're building a home, they're building a family and there's nothing more beautiful. Despite all the pain and the insane journey we've been through this year. They've won."

Their rehabilitation at Sheba Medical Center has been intensive, involving daily physical therapy, occupational therapy, and psychological support. The process of learning to use prosthetic limbs is grueling, requiring immense physical and mental fortitude. Yet Gali and Ben have approached it with determination and even moments of humor.

Their story has touched many in Israel and beyond, serving as a powerful reminder of the resilience of the human spirit and the enduring power of love. In the face of unimaginable trauma, Gali and Ben have chosen to focus on life, on their future, and on each other. Their journey of recovery is far from over, but they face it together, step by step, with hope and determination.

A SOLDIER'S BATTLE: SHLOMO KLEIN

While Gali and Ben's story unfolded at a music festival, Shlomo Klein's tale of survival and recovery began at a military outpost on the Gaza border. A member of the elite Sayeret Nachal unit, Klein was stationed at Mutzav Sufa when the Hamas assault began on October 7.

As sirens blared that morning, Klein and his comrades found themselves suddenly thrust into a desperate battle. "Our *mefaked* (commander) told us there were terrorists breaking into the base, and we ran across the base to engage them," Klein recounted. What followed was a harrowing firefight against overwhelming odds.

Klein estimates that he engaged with about 15 of the 60 Hamas terrorists who had infiltrated the base. The intensity of the combat was unlike anything he had experienced in training. "We ran into the dining room, and the terrorists were on the other side of the wall," he recalled. As he steeled himself to confront the enemy, a grenade exploded nearby, peppering his back with shrapnel.

The most devastating moment came when Klein's friend and fellow soldier, Hallel Sa'adon, was killed beside him. In an instinctive act of loyalty, Klein reached out to pull his friend's body back, not wanting the terrorists to take it. It was at this moment that a bullet struck Klein's lower right arm.

"I pulled back, and started screaming at my friend to apply a tourniquet above my elbow, to cut off the blood flow to ensure I don't bleed to death," Klein said. The pain was excruciating, compounded by the tight tourniquet that was saving his life. For the next five hours, Klein fought to stay conscious and continue defending his position, despite his severe injury.

The ordeal was far from over. As Klein and the surviving soldiers waited for reinforcements, they endured a relentless barrage of grenades - about 15 in total. "Each time I would protect my head with my left hand, say *Shema*, and be very thankful I was still alive after the explosion. As it was Simchat Torah, I sang Simchat Torah songs to myself, and even *leined* to myself the parts of my *Bar Mitzvah parasha* that I remembered by heart."

When rescue finally came in the form of Shayetet 13 (Navy Seals) forces, Klein was barely conscious due to blood loss and pain. The evacuation was chaotic, with wounded and dying soldiers piled into vehicles. It wasn't until nine hours after he was shot that Klein finally received medical attention at Soroka Hospital.

The extent of Klein's injuries became clear in the days that followed. The prolonged use of the tourniquet had caused significant damage, and his kidney function was compromised due to the buildup of toxins. Over the next few weeks, Klein underwent a series of surgeries - seven in total - to save his arm and address the various complications from his wound.

Klein's road to recovery has been long and arduous. Transferred to Sheba Medical Center for rehabilitation, he faced the daunting task of regaining function in his severely damaged arm. Progress came through small, hard-won victories. "On January 11, I moved my right bicep independently for the first time. On January 28, I moved my right wrist for the first time," Klein shared. It wasn't until the end of March, nearly six months after his injury, that he reached the milestone of being able to pick up a cup and take a drink of water independently.

Throughout his recovery, Klein has drawn strength

from the support of his family, fellow soldiers, and the broader Israeli community. His journey has also been marked by a sense of purpose that extends beyond his own healing. In March 2024, still undergoing rehabilitation, Klein traveled to the United States as part of a delegation of wounded IDF soldiers organized by the Belev Echad organization.

During this trip, Klein and his fellow soldiers visited university campuses, including UCLA, where they shared their stories with Jewish students facing rising antisemitism. For Klein, this opportunity to support others even as he continued his own recovery was deeply meaningful. "The visit to the university did more than strengthen the students; it strengthened us soldiers," he reflected. "Although physically we cannot fight on the battlefield, we can fight in other ways, such as strengthening the students on campus."

Klein's story is a testament to the physical and mental resilience required of soldiers, not just in battle, but in the long process of recovery that follows. His journey from the desperate fight at Mutzav Sufa to speaking with students in America highlights the ongoing nature of service and sacrifice, even after the immediate danger has passed.

As Klein continues his rehabilitation, he carries with him the memory of those who didn't survive, and particularly his friend Hallel Sa'adon. His recovery is not just a personal journey but a tribute to their sacrifice and a commitment to the values he fought to defend.

FROM CAPTIVITY TO ADVOCACY: MIA SCHEM

The story of Mia Schem's recovery is unique among our three tales, as it also represents the journey from captivity to freedom and advocacy. Schem, a 21-year-old French-Israeli, was among those abducted from the Supernova music festival on October 7, beginning a 54-day ordeal as a hostage in Gaza.

Schem's nightmare began when she and a friend attempted to flee the festival in her car as the Hamas attack unfolded. "I hit the gas to try and pass them but they shot the tires and the car stopped," she recounted. In the chaos that followed, Schem was shot in the arm at close range by a Hamas terrorist. "I was on the floor, covered in blood, and I screamed, 'I lost my hand, I lost my hand.'"

Critically wounded and in shock, Schem was dragged into Gaza by her captors. Her journey into captivity was a blur of pain and fear. "I didn't understand what was going on. I just told myself that I didn't want to die," she said. For three days, she was left with her injured arm tied up on a piece of plastic, fearing amputation.

Schem's captivity was marked by physical pain, psychological torment, and constant uncertainty. She underwent surgery on her arm without proper anesthesia and was forced to change her own bandages and perform physiotherapy on herself. Beyond the physical challenges, she endured emotional abuse from her captors, including being forced to film propaganda videos and endure taunts about potentially spending years in captivity.

The psychological toll of her captivity was immense.

Schem described feeling like "an animal at the zoo," constantly watched and harassed by her captors. "There's a terrorist, who is watching you 24/7, who is raping you with his eyes... an evil stare. I was afraid of being raped. It was my biggest fear there," she shared.

Despite the horrors she endured, Schem found ways to maintain hope and resilience. She recounted small acts of defiance, like waving her distinctively tattooed hands out of windows when possible, hoping to be spotted by potential rescuers. Even in her darkest moments, she clung to the belief that she would eventually be freed.

Schem's release came on November 30th, during a temporary ceasefire between Israel and Hamas. Her return to freedom, however, marked the beginning of a new challenge - recovery from the physical and psychological trauma of her captivity.

In the months following her release, Schem has undergone extensive medical treatment and rehabilitation for her injured arm. Her family reported that she has developed epilepsy as a result of the trauma and lack of sleep during her eight weeks as a hostage. The road to physical recovery has been long and difficult, involving multiple surgeries and ongoing therapy.

But perhaps even more challenging has been Schem's psychological recovery. Like many former hostages, she has had to grapple with the aftereffects of prolonged captivity, including post-traumatic stress disorder (PTSD) and difficulty readjusting to normal life.

In a remarkable display of resilience, Schem has channeled her traumatic experiences into advocacy for the hostages still held in Gaza. Despite her ongoing recovery, she embarked on a whirlwind tour of the United States in March 2024, just months after her release. This tour took her from the halls of Congress to the glamor of the Oscars, all in service of raising awareness about the plight of the remaining hostages.

Schem's advocacy began with a promise she made to her fellow captives in the final days of her imprisonment. Before her release, she vowed to the other hostages that she would "make a huge *balagan* (a great ruckus)" upon her return to draw attention to their plight. Her U.S. tour was the fulfillment of that promise.

In Washington D.C., Schem met with dozens of members of Congress from both parties, sharing her story and urging action on behalf of the remaining hostages. She attended the State of the Union address as a special guest of House Speaker Mike Johnson, using the high-profile event to keep the hostage issue in the public eye.

From there, Schem traveled to Los Angeles, where she attended the Oscars and Elton John's Oscar party, leveraging the celebrity spotlight to advocate for the hostages. Her final stop was New York, where she and her family spoke to a packed auditorium at Yeshiva University's Stern College for Women, drawing the largest crowd in the school's history.

Throughout her tour, Schem's message was clear and consistent - the world must not forget about the hostages still held in Gaza. Her personal testimony, delivered with raw honesty and emotion, put a human face on the ongoing crisis and galvanized support for continued efforts to secure the hostages' release.

Schem's journey from captivity to international advocacy in such a short span of time is a testament to her extraordinary resilience and determination. Even as she continues to grapple with her own trauma and recovery, she has found purpose and healing in fighting for others.

In her public appearances, Schem has been candid about the ongoing challenges she faces. She speaks of nightmares, of struggling with crowds and loud noises, of the constant reminders of her ordeal. Yet she also speaks of hope and of the strength she draws from her family and the broader Jewish community.

This ability to find moments of humanity even in the darkest circumstances has been a key part of Schem's resilience. It has allowed her to process her trauma without being consumed by anger or bitterness.

At the same time, Schem has been unflinching in her descriptions of the brutality she witnessed and experienced. Her testimony provides a sobering reminder of the ongoing threat posed by Hamas and the urgent need to secure the release of the remaining hostages.

As Schem continues her recovery and advocacy work, she embodies the complex journey faced by many survivors of the October 7 attacks. Her story, Gali and Ben's journey, and Shlomo Klein's recovery is one of trauma and resilience, personal healing and public advocacy, and individual suffering and collective responsibility. Ultimately, they are models of heroism.

CHAPTER EIGHT

HEROIC AMONG THE NATIONS: THE NON-JEWISH SUPPORTERS OF ISRAEL

Now, since I have shown loyalty to you, swear to me by Hashem
that you, in turn will show loyalty to my family.
Provide me with a reliable sign.
(Joshua 2:12)

"Israel continue to live! Choose life and remain faithful
to the one who brings you into His shalom. The G-d of
Abraham Isaac and Jacob lives and so do his people"
–Nate Buzolic

Though directed against the Jewish state, the Hamas attack of October 7 deeply affected supporters of Israel all across the world. From foreign aid workers who came to Israel seeking work and financial stability to vocal pro-Israel advocates who selflessly joined the Israeli Defense Forces, October 7 left no one unscathed.

FOREIGN CAREGIVERS: VIGNETTES OF COURAGE UNDER FIRE

Camille Jesalva: A Split-Second Decision

Camille Jesalva, a Filipina caregiver in Israel, demonstrated remarkable bravery during the attacks on October 7. Living in Kibbutz Nirim, near the Gaza Strip, she was caring for 95-year-old Nitza Hefetz when terrorists infiltrated the kibbutz. When one of them entered the safe room, shining his cellphone flashlight into the dark, Jesalva faced him directly.

"Hello, sir," she greeted him calmly.

"Where is the money?" he demanded.

Without hesitation, Jesalva retrieved her wallet and handed over NIS 1,500 ($375), her entire savings - a savings she had carefully been putting aside for an upcoming trip to the Philippines. "Please, sir, don't take my passport or my ticket for my flight," she pleaded.

"Is there more money?" the terrorist pressed.

"No," Jesalva answered firmly.

After he ransacked the house, she escorted him to the door. "Thank you, sir. I am closing the door now," she said.

Jesalva's quick thinking and composed actions prevented what could have been a devastating outcome for both her and Hefetz.

Ronel Gacita and Cecilia Pidalaon

Ronel Gacita had been working in Israel for eight years when Hamas attacked on October 7. As a caregiver in Efrat, a town in Judea and Samaria, Gacita has witnessed various conflicts throughout her tenure, but describes the attack on October 7 as the most severe she has ever experienced. Despite the fear and uncertainty brought about by the Hamas attacks, which resulted in significant casualties and hostages among the community of foreign workers in Israel, Gacita remains steadfast in her duties. She had initially planned to return to the Philippines but now finds herself delaying those plans. Gacita's deep gratitude towards Israel, which she now considers a second home, reflects the complex relationships many foreign workers develop with their host country. She draws strength from her faith to navigate these challenging times, mirroring the resilience shown by many foreign workers in Israel's agriculture and caregiving sectors.

Cecilia Pidlaoan, another foreign caregiver working in Jerusalem, has become a symbol of dedication and love in a time of heightened tension. Pidlaoan cares for an elderly woman who relies heavily on her support. Her unwavering commitment to her role, despite the war and pleas from her family to return home, echoes the experiences of many foreign workers in Israel. The bond that forms between caregivers and their employers, which Pidlaoan describes as a sacred duty, highlights the deep personal connections that often develop in these professional relationships. This sense of responsibility is particularly apparent in the resumption of Thai agricultural workers coming to Israel after an eight-month hiatus following the October attacks. Like many Thai workers drawn to Israel by higher wages and economic opportunities, Pidlaoan's story underscores the significant role foreign workers play in Israel's economy and society. Her dedication, along with that of thousands of others, demonstrates the resilience and commitment of foreign workers who continue to serve in various capacities across Israel, even as the country works to ensure their safety in an increasingly complex geopolitical landscape.

Ultimately, these foreign workers exhibit a quiet heroism, choosing to stay and care for others despite personal risk and the option to leave. Their decision to continue their vital work in a war zone, supporting Israel's most vulnerable, demonstrates extraordinary courage and selflessness. By prioritizing their duties over their own safety, they embody the best of human nature in times of crisis.

Nathaniel Buzolic: An Unexpected Advocate

Nathaniel Buzolic, a 40-year-old Australian actor known for his role in "The Vampire Diaries," has emerged as an unexpected and influential advocate for Israel. His journey from Hollywood heartthrob to outspoken supporter of the Jewish state offers a compelling narrative of personal transformation and dedication.

Buzolic's connection to Israel began in earnest with his first visit to the country in 2017. This wasn't just a casual tourist trip; it was a profound spiritual journey that would reshape his worldview. Before this, in 2016, while grappling with personal challenges, Buzolic had volunteered in Iraq, where he experienced what he describes as a spiritual awakening.

"In a dusty field in Iraq, Hashem came to me and said, 'If you're that willing to give up your life, give it up to me, what's the difference?'" Buzolic shared at an event at Sydney's Central Synagogue. This experience led him to study the Torah and the New Testament, ultimately drawing him to Israel.

What started as a curiosity quickly evolved into a calling. Buzolic has now visited Israel 26 times, with each visit deepening his connection to the land and its people. His advocacy took on new urgency following the October 7 Hamas attacks on Israel.

Buzolic spent a month in Israel after the attack, playing a crucial role on the ground by interviewing Israeli survivors, family members, wounded soldiers, and even former Prime Minister Naftali Bennett. He used his Instagram account, with 3.4 million followers, as a platform to share these stories and provide context to the conflict.

Recognizing the power of social media in shaping narratives, Buzolic has actively engaged in online discussions about Israel since 2021. He helped found Rova Media, and is aiming to create engaging content for younger audiences "being seduced by what's out there," as Buzolic puts it.

"I've seen Israel's failed attempts to try and stand up against the lies and propaganda of Hamas," Buzolic stated. "I think Israel's been on the defensive for so long — as opposed to the offensive — online."

Buzolic's advocacy extends beyond social media. In January 2024, he threw his support behind the "With You at Home" project, an initiative to help wives of IDF reservists who are struggling with childcare and employment while their husbands are away fighting. He participated in a volunteer recruitment campaign, visiting the homes of reservists' wives and sharing their stories.

Buzolic's efforts have not gone unnoticed. In December 2023, Rabbi Levi Wolff of Sydney's Central Synagogue bestowed upon him the title 'Righteous Among the Nations' and presented him with a menorah as a symbol to keep shining the light.

His impact has also reached the highest levels of the Israeli government. In May 2024, Buzolic was chosen to participate in the lighting of a memorial for Israel's Independence Day, an honor initiated by Israeli Minister Miri Regev.

Buzolic's advocacy has come at a personal cost. He has faced online hate, death threats, and even estrangement from some family members. He's had to arrange his own security and at one point had to put his mother into hiding.

Despite these challenges, Buzolic remains committed to his cause. "My love for the Jewish people and my love for Israel has now been galvanized," he said. "No matter what happens, no matter the cost, I will support this nation until my last breath."

Buzolic's story continues to evolve as he uses his platform to advocate for Israel and challenge prevailing narratives in the ongoing conflict. He is a true hero, standing up for truth and light despite the obstacles and dangers in his way.

Urija Bayer: A Life of Service and Sacrifice

In the rolling hills of northern Israel, the town of Ma'alot-Tarshiha bears witness to an extraordinary tale of devotion, sacrifice, and the unexpected bonds that can form between people of different faiths and nationalities. At the center of this story is Sergeant First Class Urija Bayer, a 20-year-old combat soldier in the Israel Defense Forces (IDF) who gave his life defending the country he called home, despite not being Jewish or even an Israeli citizen.

Urija's story begins not with his own birth, but with the arrival of his grandparents in Israel in the late 1960s. Hans and Crystal Bayer, German Christians, came to the Holy Land with a mission - not to proselytize or convert, but to serve and comfort. Driven by a desire to make amends for the horrors of the Holocaust perpetrated by their countrymen, the Bayers established a guest house in Shavei Zion, which is located in Northern Israel, that offered free stays to Holocaust survivors and their families. This act of compassion laid the foundation for a multigenerational commitment to serving the people of Israel.

Urija's parents, Nelly and Gideon Bayer, continued this legacy of service by running Bet Eliezer, a nursing home for Holocaust survivors in Ma'alot-Tarshiha. The facility, funded by a German-Christian charity organization called Zedakah, is staffed entirely by Christian volunteers from Europe who live alongside the residents. It was in this unique environment, where compassion and cross-cultural understanding were daily practices, that Urija and his siblings were raised.

The Bayer family's commitment to Israel has gone even beyond providing care for the elderly. Despite being non-Jewish and ineligible for Israeli citizenship, all of the Bayer children chose to volunteer for service in the IDF, with many opting for combat roles. This decision reflects a profound level of dedication to their adopted homeland, a willingness to put their lives on the line for a country that, legally speaking, was not their own.

Urija, the fourth of five children, embodied this spirit of service from a young age. Described by his parents as quiet and sensitive, he had a deep appreciation for nature and a keen desire to help others. His mother recounts how, as a child, he would bring her yellow flowers and once insisted on helping an ant carrying a heavy stick. These small acts of kindness foreshadowed the ultimate sacrifice he would make for his adopted country.

In the IDF, Urija found his calling. After attending a pre-army military academy, he blossomed, taking on additional responsibilities and excelling in his duties. He was awarded citations for excellence on two occasions and eventually joined the elite Maglan commando unit. His parents, though initially hesitant about their children serving in the military, came to see it as part of God's plan for their family.

On October 7, Urija, along with his siblings, was

called up to active duty. On December 14, during a battle in the southern Gaza Strip, Urija was severely wounded. He succumbed to his injuries on December 17, at the age of 20.

The response to Urija's death revealed the deep impact he and his family had made on Israeli society. Thousands attended his funeral, including dignitaries such as the German ambassador and high-ranking military personnel. The outpouring of grief and gratitude came from all corners of Israeli society, transcending religious and ethnic boundaries. Even ultra-Orthodox Jewish media outlets praised Urija's heroism and sacrifice.

This widespread recognition speaks to the unique position the Bayer family occupies in Israel. As German Christians serving in Israel, they represent a bridge between two communities with a painful shared history. Their dedication to serving Holocaust survivors and their willingness to defend Israel militarily have earned them respect and admiration from many Israelis.

The Bayer family's story challenges conventional notions of identity and belonging. They are neither Jewish nor Israeli citizens, yet they have integrated themselves deeply into Israeli society and culture.

This sense of responsibility to the land of Israel is shared by other German Christians who have chosen to serve Israel. Juergen Buehler, president of the International Christian Embassy in Jerusalem, estimates that there are around 100 Evangelical Christian volunteers in the Israeli army. Many of these, like the Bayer children, were born in Israel and consider it their home. For some, serving in the IDF is a way of making amends for the actions of their ancestors during the Holocaust.

The Bayer family's approach to their mission in Israel is rooted in their interpretation of biblical teachings. They see their work as fulfilling the prophecy from Isaiah: "Comfort, oh comfort My people, Says your God" (Isaiah 40:1). This verse guides their actions, from caring for Holocaust survivors to defending the country militarily. Their faith, rather than separating them from Israeli society, has driven them to integrate and serve.

When discussing their son's death, Urija's parents display a remarkable blend of grief and faith. They speak of their belief that God makes no mistakes, even as they struggle to understand the loss of their son. This perspective reflects their profound faith and their commitment to the path they believe God has set for them in Israel.

The impact of Urija's sacrifice extends beyond his immediate family and community. His story has resonated across Israel, prompting discussions about the nature of service, sacrifice, and belonging. It challenges Israelis to reconsider their perceptions of who can be considered a defender of their nation and what it means to be part of Israeli society.

When religious and ethnic tensions often dominate headlines, the heroic tale of a German Christian giving his life for Israel, of a celebrity social media influencer, and of the foreign aid workers who selflessly protect those who they love, offer a powerful example of what it looks like to be a different kind of Hero. It's only through these acts that we can build bridges and mutual understanding.

We can and we should stand together, should to shoulder.

CHAPTER NINE

HEROIC STORIES OF SALVATION

But Moses said to the people, "Have no fear! Stand by, and witness the deliverance which Hashem will work for you today; for the Egyptians whom you see today you will never see again. (Exodus 14:13)

"If there's one person in Ofakim who could charm even Hamas terrorists, then it's Rachel Edri." –Itzik Me'alem

In the darkest moments of crisis, some individuals rise to extraordinary heights of courage. The October 7 Hamas attacks on Israel and their aftermath saw countless acts of heroism, as civilians and soldiers alike put their lives on the line to save others. This chapter will dive into three remarkable stories of salvation - the sacrifice of Arnon Zmora, who was part of rescue operation of hostages from Gaza, the quick thinking of Rachel Edri in Ofakim, and the bravery of the all-women tank crews who battled terrorists on the 7th of October. Their actions not only saved lives but also inspired a nation in its hour of need.

THE ULTIMATE SACRIFICE: ARNON ZMORA'S HEROIC RESCUE

On June 8, 2024, Chief Inspector Arnon Zmora made the ultimate sacrifice in a daring mission to rescue Israeli hostages held by Hamas in Gaza. Zmora, an officer in the elite Yamam counter-terrorism unit, was critically wounded during the operation and later succumbed to his injuries. His death came in service of a higher cause - the successful rescue of four Israeli hostages who had been held captive for eight months in the hellish grip of Hamas.

The mission, which would later be renamed "Operation Arnon" in Zmora's honor, targeted a location in central Gaza where Hamas was holding Almog Meir Jan, Andrey Kozlov, Shlomi Ziv, and Noa Argamani. These individuals were among the approximately 250 people taken hostage during Hamas's brutal October 7 assault on southern Israel. For their families and loved ones, the preceding months were an agonizing ordeal of uncertainty and fear.

Zmora and his fellow Yamam operatives had trained intensively for this moment. In the weeks leading up to the operation, Zmora told his father Reuven that he was preparing for a hostage rescue mission and had a "good feeling" about their chances of success. This optimism was tempered by a clear-eyed understanding of the risks involved. A week before the mission, Zmora gave his father his watch, telling him to give it back when he returned - a poignant gesture that hinted at the dangers ahead.

When the rescue operation was launched, Zmora was among the first to breach the building where the hostages were being held. In the ensuing firefight with Hamas terrorists, he was critically wounded while providing cover for his comrades and the hostages. Despite being gravely injured, Zmora continued to fight, allowing the rest of the team to complete the extraction of all four hostages. He was evacuated to Sheba Medical Center in Tel Aviv but tragically died of his wounds shortly after arrival.

The success of the mission came at a terrible cost, but Zmora's sacrifice ensured that four Israeli citizens would return home to their families. His parents, Reuven and Ruthi, while devastated by their loss, found some comfort in knowing that their son had given his life in service of such a noble cause.

"The whole country has taken it very hard because Arnon really gave up his life knowingly to save hostages," Reuven Zmora told The Daily Mail in an interview. "People we have never met said to me they came to find out who is the family who raised this boy, to say thank you, and to say sorry for our loss."

At Zmora's funeral, attended by thousands, including top government and military officials, his mother Ruthi spoke to the father of Noa Argamani, one of the rescued hostages. "I told him that I'm very glad that Noa came back – and I hope she will live a full life, build a home and live every day like it's the last day," she recounted. This sentiment - that the rescued hostages should embrace life to its fullest - became a recurring theme in how the Zmoras processed their grief.

"This is the most important thing for us, that they really live their lives," Ruthi Zmora said. "Because this is the meaning of our loss. It was their life that motivated Arnon that day."

The Zmoras' grace in the face of tragedy touched many Israelis. Their ability to find meaning in their son's sacrifice and to express joy for the rescued hostages exemplifies the resilience and compassion that has helped sustain the country through dark times.

Arnon Zmora's heroism was not limited to his final mission. On October 7, he was among the security forces who fought to repel Hamas terrorists at Kibbutz Yad Mordechai, preventing the attack from spreading further north toward more populous areas. Throughout his career in the Yamam unit, he participated in numerous high-risk operations to protect Israeli civilians.

Yet for those who knew him best, Zmora was far more than just a warrior. His wife Michal wrote a touching tribute on social media: "The image of the hero, Arnon Zmora, may he rest in peace, is now everywhere. But long before he was a fighter and a hero, he was a sweet and charming man. An amazing partner, a perfect father. A loving and beloved man. That's how we will remember him, and I'll be glad if you do, too."

His sister-in-law, Yael Bronstein, added another dimension to the portrait of Zmora: "My brother-in-law was a true hero, a warrior who saved lives with his bare hands many times. Then he would come to our house, and we would talk about ordinary stuff and laugh, and he would scold me for being addicted to my phone when we were together, all that kind of stuff. Arnon was a man with a huge heart, so sensitive and loving. He really was an emotional person, pure gold."

This tender side of Zmora's personality aligned with his parents' description of his motivations. "Arnon hated violence or bullies and he didn't go there to kill anyone – but to save lives," his father Reuven emphasized. His mother Ruthi added: "Arnon said rescuing a hostage is the most ethical and valuable action there is."

In the aftermath of the rescue operation and Zmora's death, his parents expressed a desire for their son's legacy to extend beyond just the name of a mission. "We don't just want Arnon's legacy to be a name of mission," Reuven Zmora said. "We want people to be like Arnon."

The story of Arnon Zmora's heroic final mission is a testament to the valor of Israel's security forces and the immense challenges they face in protecting civilians and rescuing hostages.In choosing to remember Zmora not just as a fallen hero but as a loving husband, father, and son, his family reminds us of the full humanity of those who make the ultimate sacrifice in service of others. Their grace in the face of loss, and their hope that the rescued hostages will live life to the fullest, stands as its own form of heroism - one that helps a grieving nation find meaning and purpose in tragedy.

RACHEL FROM OFAKIM: COURAGE AND CUNNING IN THE FACE OF TERROR

While Arnon Zmora's heroism came in the context of a military operation, one of the most remarkable stories of salvation from October 7 involves a civilian grandmother who used quick thinking and nerves of steel to survive a harrowing hostage situation. Rachel Edri, a 65-year-old resident of Ofakim in southern Israel, found herself in an unimaginable situation when Hamas terrorists invaded her home during the early morning assault.

For many, long and agonizing hours, from Saturday morning until early Sunday, Rachel and her husband David were held captive in their own home by five heavily armed Hamas fighters. In a display of remarkable composure and cunning, Rachel managed not only to keep herself and her husband alive but also to assist in their eventual rescue by Israeli security forces.

Rachel's strategy was as simple as it was brave. She decided to treat her captors with politeness and hospitality, all while surreptitiously gathering intelligence and signaling to rescuers outside. She served the terrorists snacks and drinks, engaged them in conversation, and even sang along with them to a Hebrew song they knew from the radio.

"I can't believe I'm alive," Rachel told the news site Walla after her release. Her survival was indeed miraculous given the brutality displayed by Hamas terrorists in other locations that day. But Rachel's actions were far more than just luck - they resulted from quick thinking and remarkable emotional control in an extremely terrifying situation.

Throughout the ordeal, Rachel constantly calculated how to stay alive while also assisting the rescue efforts she hoped were underway. She repeatedly asked to use the bathroom, knowing that this would allow snipers watching the house to confirm her presence inside. When the terrorists discovered evidence that her sons were police officers, she quickly lied, saying they had emigrated to the United States - a fabrication designed to please the Hamas fighters, who often fantasize about Jewish flight from Israel.

Rachel also managed to convey crucial information to the forces outside. She flashed five fingers several times through a window, signaling the number of terrorists inside the house. This intelligence proved invaluable when police finally stormed the building in the early hours of Sunday morning.

The rescue operation was swift and effective. Police first threw in a stun grenade, at which point David Edri, despite being a heart patient, threw himself on top of his wife to shield her from any further explosions. The police team then moved in and quickly neutralized all five terrorists.

In the aftermath of her ordeal, Rachel's calm demeanor and strategic thinking drew widespread praise and even wonder from her fellow Israelis. Her story went viral, offering a rare moment of joy amid the flood of tragic news emerging from the October 7 attacks.

Rachel's actions not only ensured her personal survival but also helped protect her community. By keeping the terrorists occupied and relatively calm in her home, she prevented them from continuing their rampage elsewhere in Ofakim. Her quick thinking and bravery likely saved numerous lives beyond her own.

In interviews after her rescue, Rachel was clear about the calculations behind her seemingly hospitable behavior. "She told me she'd fed them because she knows a hungry man is more dangerous than a recently fed one," Itizk Me'alem, a neighbor of the Edris recounted. "She also knew these young men believed they would die and were probably missing their mothers. It was not a bad idea to become that person."

The story of "Rachel from Ofakim," as she came to be known across Israel, resonated deeply with a public searching for points of light amid the darkness of the October 7 attacks. Her blend of traditional Jewish hospitality with steely resolve and strategic thinking embodies something essential about the Israeli spirit.

In the days and weeks that followed, Rachel's story took on a life of its own in Israeli popular culture. Memes, cartoons, and even merchandise featuring her likeness proliferated. While some worried that this risked trivializing her ordeal, for many Israelis, it represented a way of processing the trauma of October 7 and celebrating the everyday heroism that had helped the country survive.

T-shirts bearing slogans like "Rachel Our Mother" (a play on the biblical matriarch Rachel) became popular. Cartoonists reimagined her as a superhero or a character in well-known movies and TV shows. An online game even allowed players to take on the role of Rachel, throwing cookies at terrorists to score points.

This pop culture phenomenon spoke to the deep impact Rachel's story had on the Israeli psyche. In a time of fear and uncertainty, her blend of warmth and cunning offered a model of resilience that many found inspiring. The fact that a grandmother with no military training had managed to outwit trained terrorists also provided a much-needed boost to morale.

For her part, Rachel remained modest about her actions. "I hosted them as best I could. I joked around with them. I played a game with them, in which they taught me a word in Arabic, and I taught them one in Hebrew," she recalled. "I did it all to stay alive. I needed to stall until the cavalry came to the rescue."

The story of Rachel Edri reminds us that ordinary people have the potential to be heroes. Her quick thinking, emotional control, and strategic actions in the face of mortal danger saved not only her own life and that of her husband but likely many others in her community as well.

In the harrowing hours of the October 7 attack, Rachel Edri demonstrated the strength and spirit that ultimately allowed Israel to weather the storm.

WOMEN WARRIORS: THE TANK CREWS WHO MADE HISTORY

While Rachel Edri's heroism came as a civilian, another group of women made history on October 7 as part of Israel's military response to the Hamas attacks. An all-female tank crew from the IDF's Paran Brigade played a crucial role in turning the tide of battle in several locations near the Gaza border, becoming the first women in the Western world to engage in tank combat.

The story of these women warriors begins in the early hours of October 7, when they were awakened at their base near the Egyptian border by news of the Hamas assault. With little time to process what was unfolding, the young soldiers - most in their early 20s - sprang into action.

Ordered to leave their positions on the Egyptian border, the tank crews charged northward through the region adjacent to Gaza. Their mission was twofold: to plug holes in the border fence where Hamas fighters had broken through and to engage terrorists who had already infiltrated Israeli territory.

Over the next 17 hours, these women would be in near-continuous combat, confronting challenges for which their training had not fully prepared them. They found themselves driving tanks on civilian roads at high speeds, engaging in urban combat within Israeli communities, and making split-second decisions that would determine life or death for both civilians and enemy combatants.

One of the tank commanders, a second lieutenant identified only as Michal, described a harrowing encounter on the approach to Kibbutz Holit: "My driver spotted two terrorists on the road and reported it. I told her to run them over. She simply ran over the terrorists and moved on, preventing another infiltration."

Upon reaching Holit, Michal's crew found the entrance gate closed and a panicked soldier shouting about terrorists inside the kibbutz. Without hesitation, they used their tank to smash through the gate and entered the community, ready to engage the enemy.

The actions of Michal's crew and the other women tank operators had a decisive impact on the course of the battle. Colonel Shemer Raviv, commander of the Paran Brigade, later told Channel 12 News: "The tank operators who came with their tanks actually broke the attack. In the two places, the tanks actually encountered the terrorists' fire, and the terrorists were mostly eliminated, and those who didn't simply run away because they realized they had no chance."

What made the performance of these tank crews particularly remarkable was that they were operating in conditions far removed from their usual training scenarios. "The soldiers, with three tanks at this stage of the attack, fought terrifically, fought in a way that they were purportedly not even trained for – they used fire inside Israeli settlements [and] drove on the roads," Col. Raviv noted.

The intensity of the combat these women faced cannot be overstated. They made life-or-death decisions in split seconds and engaged enemies at close range in unfamiliar terrain. One of the tank commanders, identified as Hila described the surreal nature of the war: "This was not a battle with human beings. There was no humanity here, and I aimed to protect people. Their aim was to kill people."

Despite the horrors they witnessed and the constant danger, the women displayed remarkable composure. Hagar, another tank crew member, said there was simply no time for fear. "You think about the civilians trapped in their homes and the people that needed us. You understand that there was no room for fear."

In several instances, they took proactive measures to clear terrorists from Israeli communities and secure breached sections of the border fence. Their aggressive and effective response played a crucial role in preventing Hamas from establishing a foothold in additional Israeli territory.

One particularly notable event occurred when a tank crew was dispatched to Kibbutz Sufa, which had been infiltrated by Hamas fighters. The women engaged in intense urban combat, using their tank's weapons systems with precision to eliminate terrorists while minimizing damage to civilian structures. Their actions were credited with saving numerous lives within the kibbutz.

Over the course of their 17-hour combat engagement, the women's tank crews are credited with killing approximately 50 terrorists and preventing the Hamas assault from penetrating further south into Israeli territory. Their actions saved many civilian lives and played a crucial role in containing the scope of the October 7 attack.

The significance of their achievement extends beyond the immediate tactical success. For years, the integration of women into combat roles - particularly in armored units - has been a subject of heated debate within Israeli society and military circles. Critics argued that women lacked the physical capabilities for such roles or that their presence would undermine unit cohesion.

The performance of these tank crews on October 7 offered a powerful rebuttal to such arguments. Lieutenant

General Herzi Halevi, the IDF Chief of Staff, addressed this directly in a meeting with the women soldiers after the battle:

"As you know, there has been an ongoing conversation in Israeli society over the past years as to whether or not women should be in combat positions. Sometimes, one needs to speak a great deal to explain something. We tried it in practice drills, we tried it in training exercises, we tried it in operations in normal times, but I think that here we received an answer without words. It's the answer that comes from performance in wartime combat."

The performance of these women warriors also highlighted the effectiveness of the IDF's training programs for female combat soldiers. Despite facing scenarios that went beyond their standard training, the tank crews adapted quickly and effectively to the rapidly changing battlefield conditions.

Colonel Raviv emphasized this point: "I think that thanks to those actions in this area, an attack further south was also prevented. After this war, it will already be clear – both the necessity and the proof of the clear ability there was here."

This concept of innovative resilience is not new to Israel. Throughout its history, Israel has often had to challenge conventional wisdom to survive in an incredibly hostile region. The success of these women warriors can be seen as part of this tradition – a pragmatic leveraging of all available human resources to defend the nation.

The soldiers themselves downplayed the gender

aspect of their achievement, focusing instead on their training and sense of duty. When asked about the historic nature of their combat role, Hila, responded: "So what? What does it matter? Did the terrorists know there were girls in the tanks? No. You think they saw Michal's hair sticking out of the helmet? No. Boys, girls — what does it matter?"

Another soldier, Tamar, echoed this sentiment: "You keep saying 'heroines' and 'historic'... I don't feel like a hero. I feel like I'm a soldier that was given a job, and I did my job. I think anyone would have done that."

The heroism displayed by Arnon Zmora, Rachel Edri, and the women's tank crews during the October 7 attacks reveals the multifaceted nature of courage. Zmora's sacrifice in the line of duty, Edri's quick-witted defiance as a hostage, and the tank crews' skilled combat performance each represent distinct forms of bravery. Their actions, born from different circumstances yet united in purpose, demonstrate how ordinary people can rise to extraordinary challenges when faced with grave danger.

CHAPTER TEN

HEROIC VOICES OF HOPE: THREE SETS OF PARENTS AND THEIR HOPE IN THE FACE OF TRAGEDY

And He said, "Take your son, your favored one, Isaac, whom you love, and go to the land of Moriah, and offer him there as a burnt offering on one of the heights that I will point out to you."
Genesis 22:2

> "I know that everything that happened is absolutely not your fault, and nobody's fault except that of Hamas, may their name be wiped out and their memory erased from the earth." –Iris Haim

Even in the darkest moments following the deadly "Black Saturday" of October 7, remarkable individuals have emerged, demonstrating extraordinary strength, compassion, and moral clarity. Their heroism is reflected in their kindness and resilience, with which they've navigated the pain of their reality. Iris Haim, Rabbi Doron Peretz, and Chaggai Luber have each lost a son since that day, yet they have responded with grace, wisdom, and a commitment to unity that inspires countless others. Their stories offer powerful lessons about resilience, forgiveness, and maintaining one's values, even in the face of unimaginable personal loss.

IRIS HAIM: A MOTHER'S FORGIVENESS

On December 15, 2023, Iris Haim received news that can only be described as a parent's worst nightmare. Her son Yotam, who had been held hostage by Hamas for over two months, was accidentally killed by IDF soldiers as he attempted to escape captivity. Yet amid her grief, Iris's response was not anger or blame but profound empathy and forgiveness.

Yotam Haim, a 28-year-old heavy metal drummer, was abducted from Kibbutz Kfar Aza during the brutal October 7 attacks. For 70 agonizing days, Iris clung to hope that her son was alive. Then came the devastating news that Yotam and two other hostages, Alon Shamriz and Samar Talalka, had emerged shirtless and waving a white flag in Gaza City, only to be tragically misidentified as a threat and shot by IDF troops. This tragic mistake occurred in part due to the complex and chaotic nature of urban warfare in Gaza, where Hamas Terrorists are known to disguise themselves as civilians and use human shields, making it extremely challenging for IDF soldiers to distinguish between combatants and non-combatants in high-stress combat situations.

After this heartbreaking mistake, many reacted with outrage and harsh criticism of the IDF. But Iris Haim took a different path. In a voice message that quickly went viral, she absolved the soldiers of blame and urged them not to hesitate in the future:

"I am Yotam's mother," she said. "I wanted to tell you that I love you very much and hug you here from afar. I know that everything that happened is absolutely not your fault and nobody's fault except that of Hamas, may their name be wiped out and their memory erased from the earth."

She went on: "I want you to look after yourselves and to think all the time that you are doing the best thing in the world... Nobody's going to judge you or be angry. Not me, and not my husband Raviv. Not my daughter Noya. And not Yotam, may his memory be blessed. And not Tuval, Yotam's brother. We love you very much. And that is all."

This remarkable message of love and absolution in the face of devastating personal loss touched hearts across Israel and worldwide. At a time when the nation was reeling, and tensions were at a fever pitch, Iris Haim's words were a balm of compassion and unity.

In subsequent interviews, Iris elaborated on her perspective. "When they came to tell us the news... the truth is that I wasn't angry at the IDF for even a minute, truly not, and my husband wasn't either," she told Channel 12 news. "Not for one minute. There was pain, there was sadness, there was huge sadness about the fact that Yotam isn't here, and we were in shock, total shock, but we weren't angry."

She revealed that she had recorded her message of support after hearing that morale among the soldiers was very low following the tragic incident. "It was very hard for them, because of the incident, and I said immediately that I needed to say something to them," Iris explained.

Perhaps most remarkably, Iris framed her son's death not as a senseless tragedy, but as an act of triumph and freedom. "Yotam went free. He left Hamas captivity," she said. "Even if he didn't make it to Israel alive, he was freed, and therefore he beat Hamas."

In the following months, Iris emerged as a powerful voice for unity and reconciliation in Israeli society. Having previously been politically active on the left, she spoke of how the October 7 attacks and its aftermath had opened her eyes to the humanity in all Israelis:

"Before October 7, I was entrenched in my own camp; I knew only people like me, who think like me, who talk like me, who look like me. I didn't know most Israelis... then my boy was kidnapped into Gaza and all of Israel stood up to help us. Something had opened up inside me. I can see the humanity in everyone; the good intentions of every person."

Iris began giving speeches across Israel and North America, calling for ending polarization and emphasizing themes of togetherness and hope. She spoke of rejecting victimhood and instead taking responsibility as citizens to heal divides:

"I realized that I am not just Yotam's mother. I am not just Iris Haim. I am a citizen of the State of Israel... I want the discourse in the State of Israel to change. Sure we can argue, but not in the manner that it's done today. Politics are very militant; we have many ex-generals in parliament. Israel wants something else, even if you can't see it right now."

On her first Memorial Day as a bereaved mother in May 2024, Iris penned a poignant essay reflecting on memory, loss and the meaning of sacrifice for one's country. She wrote of the intertwining of personal and national memory:

"I have a private memory, a memory of me with my son – laughing, crying, working, hugging his mother tightly. This memory is embedded in me. Memories of voices and conversations, Yotam calling me 'Mamo', coming home with another new tattoo while holding Bepanthen cream and asking shyly: 'Mom, put some on for me.' Memories of physical touch that no one can take from me.

And in the same breath, I also have a national memory. The memory of all the beloved people who lost their lives at a young age, while defending our homeland. A memory that we have a homeland, a memory that once we didn't. A memory that once there was no army to protect us, a memory that now there is. A memory to give thanks every day for the right to live here, and also to die here, because we have no other place."

Iris Haim's journey from grief to grace, from loss to a message of unity and hope, reminds us that even amidst tragedy, we have a choice in how we respond - and that choosing love and forgiveness can be a powerful force for healing.

Rabbi Doron Perez: Faith Amidst Uncertainty

For Rabbi Doron Perez and his family, the aftermath of October 7th brought a rollercoaster of emotions - from fear to hope, joy to grief, often all intermingled. Their story is one of maintaining faith and choosing to embrace life even in the face of devastating uncertainty.

Rabbi Perez is the Chairman of the World Mizrachi Movement, a religious Zionist organization. Two of his sons found themselves in the thick of the fighting on that fateful Saturday morning. Yonatan, a company commander in the Paratroopers Brigade, rushed to Sderot when the attack began. For six harrowing hours, he engaged in gun battles with terrorists, miraculously escaping with only a minor leg wound when he was shot.

Meanwhile, Daniel, a tank commander, was positioned with his unit at Nachal Oz - one of the sites overrun by Hamas fighters. In the chaos of the attack, Daniel's fate became unclear. His tank was found days later, damaged by an RPG, with one unidentified body inside. Daniel himself was classified as missing in action.

Thus began an agonizing period of uncertainty for the Perez family. Unlike families of confirmed hostages or casualties, they had no clarity on Daniel's fate. "We are hoping that he was only lightly wounded, and wherever he is, he's well and strong along with his crew," Rabbi Perez said in an interview, clinging to hope.

Yet even as they grappled with this painful limbo regarding Daniel, the Perez family faced another momentous event - the wedding of Yonatan, their eldest son, scheduled to take place only days after the October

7 attack. With heavy hearts, they decided to proceed with the wedding.

Rabbi Perez explained the decision: "If you would have told me that this is a scenario we, or any family, would have to deal with, and can deal with in a so to speak normal way, I wouldn't have believed it, but we were somehow able to do it. I think for me, the thing that gave me the strength to do it was the fact that Yonatan himself fought in the battles on the border and himself could have been killed, time and time again, and the fact that he was only wounded lightly, is an unbelievable miracle."

He continued: "The fact that Yonatan could be hopping on one leg at his wedding, in that state, was an unbelievable miracle, so that's something we're incredibly grateful for."

The wedding became a powerful symbol of hope and continuity in the face of national tragedy. Rabbi Perez reflected: "When I reflect on it, I think we are an unbelievable people. The people who may have suffered more than anyone else. Even in the horrendous suffering in Egypt, the sages tell us how Yoheved and Amram brought children to the world and Moses was born. We know that during the Holocaust, there were heroic stories of people who had children, and therefore, we come from a family of Jewish people who have faced much bigger things than our family is facing. We move on; we believe in life, I think our people believe in life more than anyone else on earth."

Tragically, the family's hopes for Daniel's safe return were not to be realized. In April 2024, after 163 agonizing days, the IDF confirmed that Captain Daniel Perez had been killed on October 7th and his body was being held captive by Hamas in Gaza.

At Daniel's funeral at Mount Herzl military cemetery in Jerusalem, attended by thousands, the Perez family buried Daniel's blood-stained uniform. Hamas continues to hold his body hostage in Gaza.

At the funeral, Rabbi Perez chose to focus on his son's heroism instead of his own grief. "We came to honor you, all the members of your team, who ran with you like lions to protect others with incredible courage... Daniel, you saved so many lives with unwavering dedication to your mission... You saved people in the Nachal Oz army base and you saved people in Kibbutz Nachal Oz. You know what, Daniel? It's possible that you saved not only generations of people you don't know, but perhaps you even saved the life of your brother, Yonatan. After all, Yonatan also fought later that day in Nachal Oz and was injured 100 yards from where you were taken. Had you not done what you did, who knows how many more terrorists may have ambushed Yonatan in the base that day."

In the aftermath of the devastating confirmation of Danie's death and the abduction of his body to Gaza, Rabbi Perez and his family maintained their dignity and faith. Their story - from Yonatan's wedding to the long vigil for Daniel and finally the grief of confirmed loss - became a microcosm of the national experience. Through it all, they heroically exemplified grace, hope, and an unwavering commitment to life and continuity.

CHAGGAI LUBER: A FATHER'S PLEA FOR UNITY

On December 25, 2023, Yehonatan Lober was killed in action in Gaza, leaving behind his pregnant wife, Aviya Lober, and their 10-month-old son. A deeply spiritual man, he was the son of Chaggai Luber, founder of the religious theater company Aspaklaria in Jerusalem. At the funeral, Chaggai eulogized his son, but also called for national unity and an end to divisive rhetoric:

"I want to say that Yehonatan is no longer just my son, he is your son. Before Simchat Torah we all went through a difficult time. We felt that our beloved nation was falling apart. The damned enemies came and reminded us that we are one nation and forced us to speak to each other and fight side by side."

In a media landscape increasingly dominated by polarization and angry protests, Chaggai has taken a different approach, becoming a powerful voice calling for national unity. He regularly stands before crowds of demonstrators holding a sign with a simple, heartfelt plea: Enough with the violent demonstrations and discourse.

This call for calm and unity comes from a place of deep pain, but also profound faith. In interviews, Chaggai has spoken movingly of his son's devotion both to religious observance and to his military service.

The incredible thing is that Chaggai sees no contradiction between deep religious faith and dedication to military service. Rather, he views his son's approach to both as stemming from the same wellspring of commitment and idealism.

In Israeli public discourse, the perception is that despite being a yeshiva student - you should enlist, despite being religious - you should be in the IDF, despite it not being a predominantly Biblical environment, a godly environment like a yeshiva - you should overcome and go to the IDF.

This perspective - seeing military service as a profound expression of religious values rather than a compromise of them - contrasts some voices in the ultra-Orthodox community who oppose IDF service. Chaggai's words offer a powerful counter-narrative that bridges the often fraught divide between secular and religious Israelis.

In the face of his own grief, Chaggai has maintained a remarkably broad and empathetic perspective. He speaks of receiving both painful and uplifting responses from people across the political and religious spectrum. Perhaps most notably, he recounted how members of "Brothers in Arms" - a left-wing organization often criticized by the religious right - visited his community of Beit El in Judea and Samaria for the first time to offer his family condolences during the seven-day mourning period.

This openness to those with different views extended to Chaggai's approach to coping with loss. Rather than focusing solely on absence and grief, he emphasizes the importance of celebrating life.

Chaggai's call for unity and an end to divisive rhetoric came at a crucial moment. As the war in Gaza dragged on and hostages remained in captivity, Israeli society began to show small signs of fracturing. Protests against the government grew increasingly heated, with some families of hostages engaging in confrontational tactics.

In this charged atmosphere, Chaggai penned a powerful open letter addressed to parents of hostages who were calling for intensified struggle against the government. With compassion but also firmness, he urged restraint:

"Nobody will burn my country. We are tired of the threats of extremists. Yes, even if these extremists have relatives in Gaza. You will not burn the country. That's out of the question. And if I have to fight you, I will fight. Millions of people look at you in disbelief, disapproval, and shock, and only out of respect for you, they are silent. I will not be silent."

He continued: "My son was killed in Gaza. He went to protect and free your children and was killed. Left everything, left behind a pregnant wife and a nine-month-old child, and was killed. He won't come back again. Not in any deal. And so I am allowed to tell you: You must not break up the country. You must not go wild. You are not allowed to block roads. You must not confront the police. You must not call for people to refuse to serve."

Chaggai's words cut through the noise of angry rhetoric, reminding Israelis on all sides of the importance of maintaining national unity and democratic norms, particularly during times of crisis. His ability to deliver this message from a place of personal loss gave it particular moral weight.

At the same time, Chaggai is careful to affirm the

right to peaceful protest and expression of differing views: "Express your opinion - but don't shout. Say that we must have an agreement now – and don't block the roads. Say an 'everyone for everyone' deal - and don't call for a rebellion."

In calling for calm and unity while still respecting democratic dissent, Chaggai offered a model for how Israelis could navigate the tensions and grief of wartime without losing their values or tearing society apart.

Iris Haim, Rabbi Doron Peretz, and Chaggai Luber each suffered devastating personal losses in the wake of October 7th. Yet in their grief, they found the strength to persevere and become heroic voices of hope, unity and moral clarity for a wounded nation.

These parents remind us of a fundamental truth: that even in our deepest grief, we can choose how we will respond to tragedy. And in that choice lies the seeds of healing for ourselves, our communities, and our world. Their examples challenge us to rise to our best selves, choose unity over division, hope over despair, and love over hate - even when, perhaps especially when, it seems most difficult.

THE HEROIC CALL – YOU CAN BE A HERO TOO

Reflecting on these narratives, it becomes clear that extraordinary acts often arise from ordinary people, and moments of crisis can transform ordinary people into heroes. When called upon to rise above the mundane, many discover an unexpected capacity for extraordinary acts.

Whether it was civilians who charged into danger to save others or parents who turned their personal grief into a source of strength for their communities, the heroes we've met in these pages have one thing in common: they acted when it mattered most.

Heroism comes in many forms, each as vital and inspiring as the next. For example, we've seen individuals like Aner Shapira, whose bravery during the massacre at the Nova music festival saved countless lives, and Iris Haim, who channeled her grief over the loss of her beloved son into acts of kindness and leadership that brought hope to those around her. Their actions remind us that heroism isn't just about physical courage; it's also about moral and emotional strength. It's about standing up for what is right, even when it's difficult or painful.

Aner's story teaches us that sometimes heroism is about seizing the moment, acting instinctively out of love and a deep-seated sense of duty. Iris's story demonstrates that heroism often emerges from personal tragedy, transforming individual grief into a force for collective good. Both forms of heroism are essential, and both have the power to change lives.

Elchanan Kalmanson didn't set out to be a hero. But when terror struck, he stood his ground. As screams filled the air and gunfire erupted, Kalmanson's voice remained steady, his hands calm. He guided terrified civilians to safety, shielding them with his own body. In the face of unimaginable horror, Kalmanson didn't run. He didn't freeze. He acted. With each life he saved, each person he comforted, Kalmanson pushed back against the tide of violence. His heroism wasn't flashy or loud. It was in his unwavering presence, his refusal to give in to fear, and his determination to protect those around him, even at the cost of his own life.

Amit Mann's bravery also offers a powerful example of how heroism can emerge from a place of deep personal conviction. Imagine the weight of mortality pressing down on her shoulders as she sat in that makeshift clinic, the metallic scent of blood mingling with antiseptic. Amit Mann knew she was staring death in the face, yet her hands never wavered as she tended to her wounded community members. With each life she fought to save, Mann defied her own impending doom. The cold grip of fear threatened to paralyze her, but she pushed through, driven by a fierce loyalty that transcended self-preservation. In those harrowing hours, Mann wasn't just a soldier or a medic – she became the very embodiment of sacrifice, choosing to spend her final moments not in despair, but in a relentless battle against the inevitable, gifting others a chance at life even as her own slipped away.

The stories of these heroes illustrate that both actions and words have the power to inspire and lead. Words can galvanize, comfort, and guide us through the darkest times. They can rally a community, as we've seen in the speeches, prayers, and messages that have echoed across the nation in the wake of October 7. But words alone are not enough. They must be backed by action—by the willingness to step forward, to take risks, to put others before ourselves.

Heroism is not an abstract concept; it's a choice we make every day. It's in the parent who reassures their child in the face of fear, in the neighbor who offers a helping hand and in the leader who speaks out against injustice. Every act of kindness, every gesture of solidarity, every stand for truth contributes to a larger tapestry of heroism that binds us together as a people.

After learning about these heroes, we must ask ourselves: How will we rise to the occasion? What will our contribution be to this ongoing story of heroism?

Heroism doesn't always mean running into the line of fire—sometimes, the fire is metaphorical. It might be standing up for someone who has no voice, speaking out against an injustice, or caring for someone in need. We all have something we're willing to risk everything for, something that touches the core of who we are and what we believe. Heroism is in the everyday decisions we make, in the way we treat others, and in the values we uphold. It's in the way we respond to adversity, the way we support our loved ones, and the way we contribute to our communities. Each of us has a role to play in the ongoing story of our people. Each of us has the power to make a difference.

The time to act is now. The challenges we face are great, but so too is our capacity for courage and compassion. The examples set by the heroes of October 7 are a reminder that we are all capable of extraordinary things. We all have the potential to be heroes, not in the sense of performing superhuman feats, but in the sense of being human in the fullest, most generous, and most courageous way possible.

The heroes of October 7 have left us with a powerful legacy—a legacy of courage, sacrifice, and unwavering commitment to the values that define us as a people. This legacy is not just theirs; it is ours as well. It is a legacy that we must carry forward, in our words, our actions, and our hearts.

As we move forward, let us remember the lessons of these heroes. Let us honor their memory by striving to live up to their example. Let us be the kind of people who rise to the occasion, who stand together in times of crisis, and who never lose sight of the power of love, courage, and community.

In the face of the challenges that lie ahead, let us find strength in each other and in the stories of those who have gone before us. Let us be inspired by their bravery, guided by their wisdom, and emboldened by their example. And let us always remember that heroism is not just about what we do in extraordinary circumstances, but about how we live our lives every day.

Now is the moment to embrace that power. Now is the moment to stand up, to speak out, and to act with courage and compassion. Now is the moment to write the next chapter in the story of our people—a chapter of hope, strength, and heroism.

SOURCES

World Mizrachi Online Newspaper
Accessed online at mizrachi.org.

YNet News, Online Newspaper
Accessed online at ynetnews.com/category/3083.

Jerusalem Post
Accessed online at jpost.com.

Times of Israel
Accessed online at timesofisrael.com.

Arutz Sheva
Accessed online at israelnationalnews.com.

Haaretz
Accessed online at haaretz.com.

Magen David Adom
Information sourced from the official
Magen David Adom website: mdais.org.

IDF Online

Information sourced from the official Israel Defense Forces website: idf.il/en/.